I0334627

Australian Road Guide

Guthugga Pipeline Press

Drive Time: Australian Road Guide
ISBN: 978-0-9942154-7-5 (paperback)
ISBN: 978-0-9942154-8-2 (hardback)

©2022 Greg Appel
Published by Guthugga Pipeline Press
Book design and production: Eddy Jokovich/ARMEDIA
Greg Appel: www.spontaneousfilms.com.au

Thanks to all who helped out with this book. Eddy Jokovich a highly creative graphic artist, an excellent mind and a fine podcast companion. Frances Green for her straight ahead advice. Liane Pfister for her solid spelling support. Claudia Taranto for giving me the chance to work on all these amazing street programs. Steve Brown for the whole streets concept! Paul Clarke for all sorts of creative encouragement. Blak Douglas for his artwork and insights. Fabian Prideaux and Fiona Edge for their help with 'pling's fantastic archive. Mark Alsop for the Oxford Street images. Word Travels and the slam poets who travel with them. Alice Pung for the Barkly Street words. The Lighthouse Keepers for all the fun.

Then there's the other musical companions: Guthugga Pipeline, Grant Brothers, Widdershins, OneHeadJet, King Curly and, let's not forget Hammerhead. My immediate family Amanda, Zelie and Anders for being a part of this road trip. My greater family – including all those in photos, a sketch of a Kombi from Mette Kragh, and especially Dad who took a few of these pictures and drove us out of that driveway into the world beyond. My tolerant friends and everyone in this for your words, time and company. The NSW and Federal Governments for their generous non-judgemental coronavirus arts funding. And, of course, you my dear reader.

 Produced from a range of sources, including ABC Radio National's *Earshot* and the *Drive Time* podcast. Listen through Apple Podcasts or your favourite podcast provider.

 A catalogue record for this work is available from the National Library of Australia

Australian Road Guide

THE BOOK

Informed by years on the road as a musician and documentary maker, this book is part memoir, road guide and a fascinating social history of Australia. Written in an accessible style, it is informed by wide ranging interviews from faded celebrities to jaded nobodies. From a range of sources including ABC Radio National's *Earshot* and the *Drive Time* podcast.

After writing a well-received memoir based on his experience in an 'eighties Australian indie band, *Confessions of a Lighthouse Keeper*, Greg Appel realised he had much more in his old boxes under the bed: photos, pamphlets and artefacts from ancient road trips illustrate this present day safari.

Beginning with his misty hometown of Canberra in the 'seventies, the reader is taken on an Australian wide odyssey of change, cuisine, culture and whatever comes around the next bend.

Eat well, sleep well, and drive on.

THE AUTHOR

Perhaps as a punishment for his sins in this indie world, Greg Appel ended up as the producer of the ABC TV rock history *Long Way to the Top* and has created numerous other music programs and events. As a guitarist/songwriter for the Lighthouse Keepers in the mid-'eighties, his interest in music has often influenced his work.

His diverse award-winning documentaries includes directing *The Team That Never Played* in 2010, an international documentary about apartheid-era football, produced by Frances Green. In 2020, he directed *Australia Come Fly with Me* for SBS TV, a three-part series about the history of the Australian aviation industry hosted by Justine Clarke.

His 2008 documentary, *Bossa Nova: the sound that seduced the world* premiered at the Sydney Film Festival and was broadcast on ABC TV. He has also produced many feature documentaries for ABC Radio National. And, of course, he is the author of *Confessions of a Lighthouse Keeper*.

CONTENTS

A DRIVING NATION — 6

CANBERRA: CONCRETE, MIST AND ROUNDABOUTS — 16

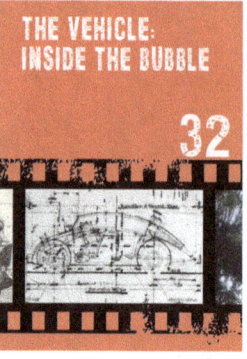
THE VEHICLE: INSIDE THE BUBBLE — 32

WHAT GOES ON THE ROAD STAYS ON THE ROAD: TARCUTTA — 43

MAURICE STREET, MALLACOOTA — 56

WENTWORTH STREET, PORT KEMBLA — 65

OXFORD STREET, SYDNEY — 73

HIGHWAY 1 REVISITED — 80

THE SUBURBS — 88

BATHURST — 99

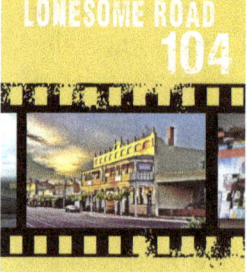
ST ARNAUD LOOK DOWN THAT LONESOME ROAD — 104

BARKLY STREET, FOOTSCRAY — 110

THE SUNSHINE STATE 119 	**HOBART** 134 	**ARGENT STREET, BROKEN HILL** 140 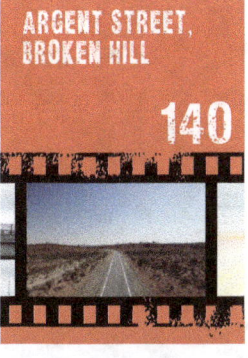	**AUSTRALIA ACROSS** 153 
ALICE SPRINGS: THE CROSSROADS 158 	**AU REVOIR AUSTRALIE** 167 	**EPILOGUE** 172 	

A DRIVING NATION

A DRIVING NATION

MUSIC
* *Walking on the Moon*, the Police
* *Peace Train*, Cat Stevens
* *Wide Open Road*, the Triffids
* *Ode to Nothing*, the Lighthouse Keepers

STAY
At The Grace Hotel in Sydney, a great place to start.

EAT
Harry's Café De Wheels, Woolloomooloo Bay. This is where good road food starts.

POINT OF INTEREST
Refresh yourself with the 'Where the bloody hell are you?' tourism campaign. An interesting point in Scott Morrison's advertising career. Although, no doubt, he didn't have much to do with it. The most likely scenario is – someone else did it, he claimed it, then he disowned it when the mood shifted. But, whatever happened – the English loved it, it's how they see their old colony.

In the entertainment industry, 'the road' has a mythic status. You hit it, it can give you fever and you're not meant to talk about what goes on there. Putting on shows for unsuspecting strangers in different towns is what it's all about. I've played my own small part by getting up on rickety stages around this country. I've also spent many years documenting other people on the road. Poets, writers, removalists, dreamers, psychics, unclassifiable performers and lots of musos.

Being a travelling minstrel is not always lucrative. The Triffids might have come up with a classic road song 'Wide Open Road' in 1986 but it didn't make them rich.

Rob McComb, the Triffids: I was trying to explain it to my son years ago when he was asking what happened to all the money. It wasn't about getting rich, we were on a quest. You know, like Frodo and his merry gang.

A journey to drop a ring into the fiery cracks of Mount Doom must be the ultimate road trip.[1] I firmly believe this book will be just as satisfying for you as it was for Frodo. Although hopefully not as tiring. What is our quest? We are seeking both pleasure and knowledge on our grand Australian road trip. A land so vast you can get lost in time and space. Our ring? It's probably one of those ring-pulls off an old fashioned tinnie. But this one has magical powers. We will revisit the days when you timed a drive by the slab of beer. The journey from Melbourne to Sydney was easily one, maybe two. No such thing as RBT. You might feel a little drunk, or is it something more? Crack one open and we're off to see the wizard.[2]

The music business can be compared to drug dealing. In fact, the two often are intertwined. There's the street dealers, who hustle out on the street, often have drug habits and can lead difficult impoverished lives. At the other end, there's the big kahunas who have a whole lot of money and may not even take drugs. In between, there's a few layers of bigger and lesser dealers, but to make money, you have to be very near the top of the chain. For the street dealer, it's always about trying to get enough together to make it to the next level. The foggy dream is to be a *kahuna*.

A very small percentage make money, and just about all of it gets channelled up to the kahunas. Apparently, it's one of the building blocks of our economy and one reason illicit drugs are still illegal.[3]

In music, most artists are hustling on the street. I certainly did my time there. I could see that just maybe, it was possible to make money and be famous. Somehow, it never quite happened. But street hustlers might buy the music and attend the concerts given by the chosen few. It all seemed so possible.

Being a street hustler meant you were also looking at the street as a route of escape. If you could get your act together and get out on the road, playing your music in other places, you just might move up a notch. A huge band, like say the Police, who were giant in the mid-eighties, could travel around the world, raking in the glory. It was all clearly visible to the underlings. In fact, me and my little gang of music enthusiasts had a close encounter in the Bruce Stadium in Canberra. We were just old enough for some of us to have licenses, so we could get to shows in our own cars, or at least the borrowed parent vehicle. The Police came to visit the antipodes at the height of their fame. While the support band were playing to the rest-

1 Although you are left wondering why they didn't just fly there on eagles, like happens elsewhere in middle earth, Nazgûl would have ripped them out of the air? Perhaps.
2 Puns on The 'Wizard of Oz', where Oz indicates Australia, have been used many times across the arts, mainly during the 1970s. So, we will resist. Except for this footnote.

3 I think I got some of this theory from Yen Yang, an arts futurist.

Photo, courtesy of Godfrey Appel (my grandfather) Caption, courtesy of Denis Appel (my father). 'This is me and Margaret about 1950. Mum and Aunty Nell with her partner Mrs Thomas. Lesbians. Nell was headmistress of Marsden Girls School in Bathurst and Mrs T followed her from school to school as housekeeper.

less mob waiting for the main act to come on, our friend Ben[4] decided to take a piss in one of the huge stadium troughs. As any male knows, there's a decorum at work in these trough situations. Don't look around or down. But Ben's eyes did glance sideways and who should be standing beside him? Sting! What a man of the people. You'd think they'd have a special toilet for a megaband, in a massive stadium. It would have been unlike Ben to study Sting's off stage appearance further, but I think Sting said something to him. I'm sure Ben snorted politely and looked stoically forward while having a very unrelaxed piss. When he got out and breathlessly told us the news, it made our trip to see the Police that much better. We could see that these people were human just like us.

4   This Ben seems to appear often in my writing. I'm sorry Ben!

At some point in life, I turned into a documentary maker and I was even paid to record people's stories. I've met many fellow travellers out there, some have shared their tales with me. I'm sometimes amazed at how willing and candid people can be in an interview situation. To this point, I have never had any of them complain about my interpretations of their stories. So let's hope it stays that way. It's been a privilege to listen.

My interviewing techniques can be quite juvenile, even in advanced years – I can never resist pushing the sex button, just to see what people say. I still find it an endlessly diverting subject. But I never regret these diversions when I watch documentaries I've been involved with, in front of an audience. Even in today's sexually awkward world.

When talking about the road, it can be hard to throw in a sex-related question. Or is it? In the conversations I had for this project, I often referred to that hoary old saying

Artwork by Blak Douglas: *How fast are you going now?*

'what goes on the road stays on the road'. But there are alternative interpretations of the travellers' credo. Blak Douglas is an artist/musician who frequently uses imagery from the mythical road in his work. His *nom de plume* 'Blak Douglas' is a play on his Indigenous and Scottish heritage.

> **Blak Douglas:** There's an obvious meaning to that phrase. But if you have the luxury of learning from a local mob about a very special place. Then that the story is meant to be retained by you. You're not meant to repeat the stories and repeat the language that belongs to that place where you receive that story. So perhaps that's a nice cultural way of looking at the phrase. Leave it there. It's like they used to say, you don't take a piece of rock from Uluru. It's gonna bite you on the bum later on.

The road isn't just about entertainers plying their trade. There's all sorts of people going back and forth. Sometimes I look at a busy road and wonder, 'where are they all going?' How could there be that much need for transportation? People look intensely invested in their destinations. Or are they just aimlessly driving about? Something I have occasionally indulged in. As the world heats up, we may have to cut down on some of these trips. Indeed, the virus proved this was possible. But it remains a big part of the Australian culture. Just keep moving. Preferably in a vehicle. And once you've got to that place, get ready to go back.

I'm the sort of driver that is largely ignorant of the complex machinery that makes the vehicle move. And I'd like it to stay that way. Whatever goes on under the bonnet, stays under the bonnet. I might just about be able to change a flat tyre but would have a lot of trouble changing a piston ring. This manual is for the ordinary driver who doesn't dwell on differential modifications.

Many of the people I've interviewed are what you might call 'ordinary people'. Some of them aren't. But dig a little deeper and everyone has a story to tell. That's why I'm inflicting mine on you. Intertwined with the ordinary and the semi-extraordinary.

I'll go back to my ordinary but privileged beginnings. It wasn't that unusual to have a family car by the time I was born in 1962, but they were still special things and they needed to live in a garage. When you think back and scratch out your earliest memories, they are distinctly foggy. I know that technically I was born in Sydney in the North Shore Hospital. But you know what? I cannot remember a thing about it.

Cars are subtly introduced to the young early in life. Young me and dad and car in UK during 1964.

My first confirmed memories actually come at the age of three, all the way from the UK where my parents lived for a while, when dad was getting his doctor qualifications. But back in Australia they start to clarify. It's very hard to separate them from the 35mm photos and Super-8 footage my father took. Filming the day-to-day drudge would be a waste of expensive footage, so the footage often involved road trips and holidays. Not everyone had cameras in those days, and we were well off enough to afford these fairly expensive items. In fact my grandfather shot 16mm colour footage way back in the 1940s. Having more than the average income was socially awkward in those days. Not so much now.

Luxury items or not, I had a happy childhood, and I think I instinctively knew that my lot was good. Looking back now – I was indeed very lucky and privileged. If it was karma from a previous life. I had been a very good person. Australia was like me. Innocent, fun, prosperous and any past darkness blocked out. But could this come back to haunt the nation? Or me?

Being the eldest of five, I found myself in my own bedroom early on. As the household population increased, the other four were paired up. This had its advantages and disadvantages. It was great to have my own space, but once the lights went out, it was just me and whatever else. It was also at the back of a long white house, and a large corner window meant the dark yard and shrubbery were close. There was plenty of rustling to make my sleep uneasy. Then there was the Australian wildlife. The first time I heard a possum's nocturnal cry was alone in my bedroom. No one had informed me of their hideous throaty rasp, and I didn't work it out for a long time. I

My sister Margie and me pose with wistful looks, dog and picnic basket, in the back of the family station wagon.

just thought some kind of devils were out there. But in the back of the family car, it felt safe, even by night with only the odd shadow in the trees to bother my psyche.

It was on these long car trips that stories were heard. I was the chief storyteller in our family, but sometimes I listened. And sometimes, there might be someone from another family travelling with us. People really did tell stories in those days. It sounds so foreign to the world we now live in.[5] Where everyone is plugged into an entertainment device.

Often, stories were passed round between young people, at suitable opportunities. When the adults were carousing or perhaps after a ouija board session in the dark. These events could easily occur simultaneously. But the ideal setting for one particular tale was in the back of a moving car on a drizzly night. It went something like this.

Let's call the happy couple Tom and Jill. They are on their honeymoon and in love. It's a wet night as they drive towards the place where honeymooners do their stuff. We didn't quite know what that was, but it was a happy place they seemed keen to get to. The rain keeps getting harder and now there's lightning cracking across the road. Branches fall. Just the right time for the car to break down.

Cars were always breaking down then. So this was all quite possible. Tom has to hitchhike to the next town to get help. Jill stays in the car with the doors locked. Tom has been gone a while, so Jill turns on the radio for comfort. She finds some soothing music, perhaps a song like 'Peace Train' by Cat Stevens. But then the news comes on. It's all about an escaped mental patient. The storyteller would insert the nearest known psychiatric institution as the place they

5   I joined my son and a group of his friends online to play *Dungeons and Dragons* not long ago. This is storytelling – what am I going on about!

escaped from. We all seemed up on these locations. Then suddenly there's a bang on the roof. Here, the storyteller might bang the car interior subtly. The listeners were getting nervous.

The story went on with rain, lightning, falling trees and ever increasing banging, 'til Tom's head appears at the window. Thank goodness! But his head is upside down and dripping blood. Jill gets out of the car and turns around to find it's the escaped lunatic with Tom's head on the roof of the car!

It's eerie to think now, that just off the road between Sydney and Canberra where we commonly travelled during these story sessions, there was a real lunatic on the loose. The Belanglo State Forest will forever be associated with Ivan Milat[6] and the backpacker murders. Nobody can say when they started for sure, but there are missing persons from as far back as the 'seventies.

I remember hitching myself in the 'eighties. It wasn't something I enjoyed, but it was much more common. Juliet Ward, who would become the singer for our band the Lighthouse Keepers, seemed to be constantly hitching with her dog Chaos, when I first met her.

Today, you hardly ever see someone with their thumb stuck out on the side of a country road. Gone is that feeling of guilt and relief as you sped past. Except if they happened to be a couple of attractive young women, then you just might have pulled over. Frances Green and Monica, her identical twin sister, were a successful duo in those days. They grew up in rural Victoria and found hitchhiking was a free ticket to the entire country during the 'seventies and 'eighties.

France Green: My sister and I hitchhiked everywhere. We used to go away for weekends, we hitchhiked up to NSW, Queensland, across the Nullarbor, Western Australia. And adventures were had. But if things got a bit hairy, we always had an agreement that we would use a secret word that we've used our entire lives, which is like a signature word to say – something's amiss. We need to respond in whatever way.

Frances sometimes had another sister join them as well, and this could cause problems with getting a ride, even with the most eager male drivers. It seemed two wasn't a problem. So two would stay on the side of the road while one hid. The car would slow down and before the driver could react, the hidden sister would appear. But no secret word or tricks could get the twins out of trouble when they got a ride near Margaret River, just south of Perth. This friendly driver didn't seem to care what the twins were up to in the back seat.

Frances Green: We had a bag of dope with us. And we rolled a joint in the car. And unbeknown to us, a police car came up towards the back of the car, then the siren and the lights started. And seeing the cops behind us, we threw the bag of dope outside the window, which the cops saw, and subsequently picked up. And then they pulled us over. And my sister and I had to declare that we were the owners of the marijuana. And that, yes, that was us, smoking dope in the back of a car.

---

6 Australia has a small enough population for one of the people interviewed in this book, to have married a woman whose brother was killed by Ivan Milat. He didn't tell me on the record, so I won't put a name to this disclosure.

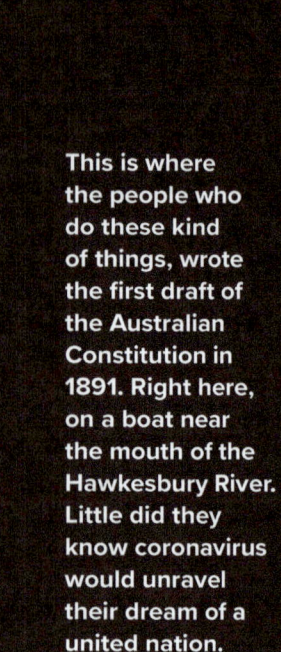

This is where the people who do these kind of things, wrote the first draft of the Australian Constitution in 1891. Right here, on a boat near the mouth of the Hawkesbury River. Little did they know coronavirus would unravel their dream of a united nation.

They ended up in jail in Busselton, and they both had to live with criminal convictions for the rest of their lives. It could make international travel difficult, even if you were a top broadcasting bureaucrat from Down Under.

Today, Western Australia remains a law-unto-itself kind of state, but Australia as we now know it, nearly didn't happen. Coronavirus has made it clear that present day Australia is made up of random borders that enclose groups of people that don't always love their neighbours. At the turn of the nineteenth century, we were forced together by a legislated Federation, to become a nation.

I learned something new about Federation on a recent trip up the Hawkesbury River that curls around Sydney.[7] Rivers were the original highways of this land and now form two of the less random borders. They were long used by Aboriginal people and then by the Europeans as they drove further inland. The Constitution for our Federation was all worked out on a boat on the Hawkesbury, full of politicians from the various British colonies that would become the states. According to our skipper, they wrote the Constitution in a day, and frolicked in the water for the other four. This information is possibly inaccurate. But, the

7 The Hawkesbury is one of the borders of the Eora nation that covers present day Sydney, the others being the Nepean (which is confusing because it joins the Hawkesbury) and the Georges River

A DRIVING NATION

@MidCuthbert: Ooh, I'm a Melbournian. I get sad when there's a lockdown. I get sad when the tennis man loses. I get horny for state officials. I eat toast in a dirty lane. I'm disappointed by the AFL. The bus is like a little train. Don't tap on in the free zone. Franco Cozzo. Ketamine.

Says 'retired finance admiral' on Twitter – that most bitchy of social medias. Will we still be a nation at the end of this road trip?!

* 🚗 *

SCANDAL RADAR

The Constitution might have been worked out in a day on the Hawkesbury (according to our skipper) but the preliminary discussions went on for almost as long as John Farnham's farewell tours in the 1990s. Constitutional conventions were held across Australia between 1891 and 1897, but Bathurst event in 1896 was the most controversial. John Norton, a keen republican, unionist and editor of *The Truth*, was opposed to the proposed Federation model and several weeks before the Bathurst event, published an article declaring Queen Victoria a 'semi-senile old woman' and the royal family as 'podgy faced lecherous bastards, bigamists and wife beating boozers'. Somehow, Norton obtained a speaking position at the convention, outlined the perils of the monarchy and the virtues of a republic. His speech threatened to derail Federation but the monarchists rejected Norton's 'ill-advised republicanism' and Australia stayed loyal to Queen and King.

---

gist of it seems to be true. After their boat meeting, Australia was proclaimed a nation on 1 January 1901 in Centennial Park, in nearby Sydney.

But we are getting distracted by water, even though it girts our nation. Hop in, we are about to embark on a land journey. By car. Around the very nation they signed off to, in their boat. It's a land with mysterious borders that were created that fateful day.

But even as I write and lockdowns start to niggle at the union of states that makes up the Federation. There are troubling signs that all do not see it that way.

CANBERRA: CONCRETE, MIST AND ROUNDABOUTS

NGUNNAWAL AND NGAMBRI COUNTRY

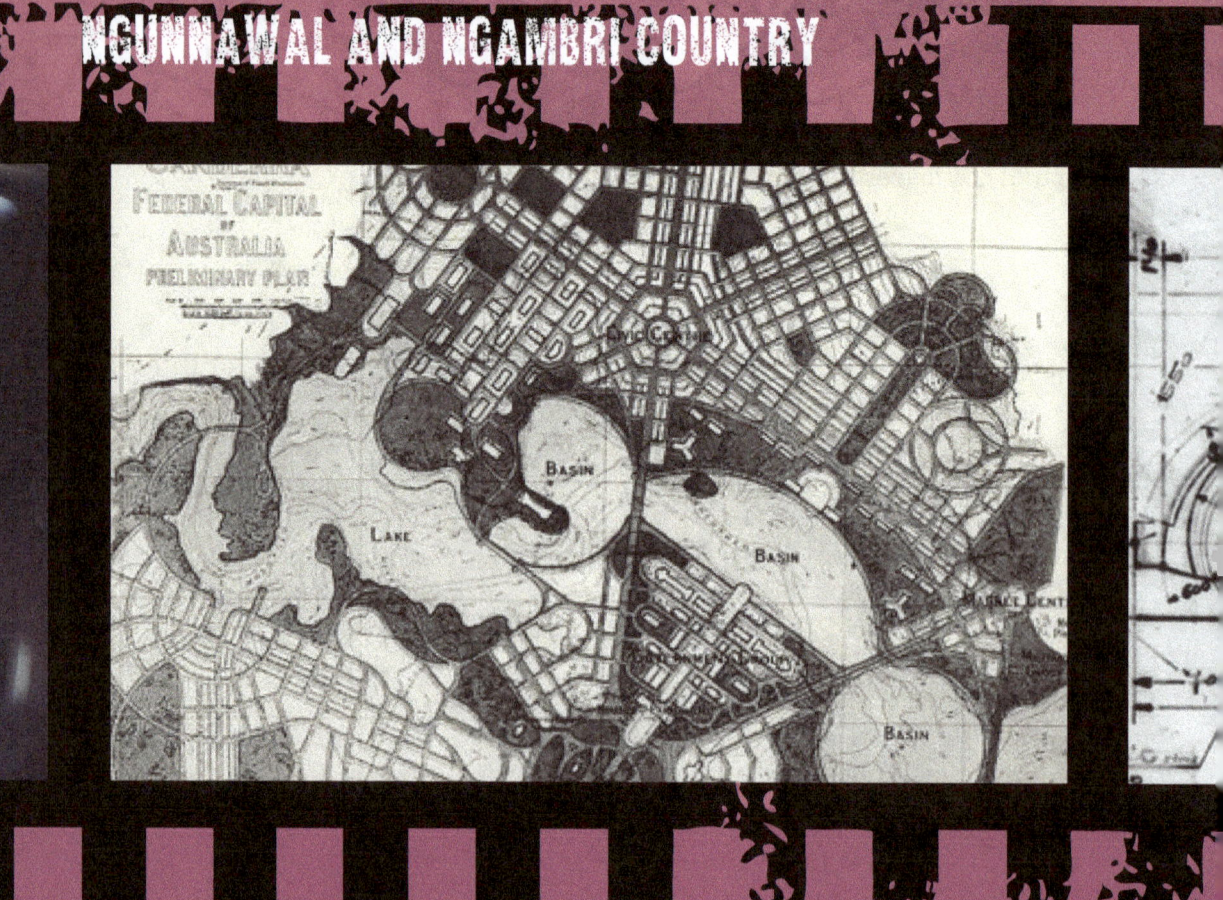

CANBERRA: CONCRETE, MIST AND ROUNDABOUTS

MUSIC
* *Funeral for a Friend/Love Lies Bleeding*, Elton John
* *Reptile*, the Church
* *Anarchy in the UK*, Sex Pistols
* *Dog Eat Dog*, Adam and the Ants
* *King Ben*, the Widdershins

STAY
At the Rex Hotel in Northbourne Avenue for an old world retro feel.

EAT
At Brodburger in Kingston.

RANDOM POINT OF INTEREST
Canberran concrete cubicle style 'Action' bus stops still come with a bold splash of orange.

VISIT
The National Portrait Gallery – these kind of places can be boring, but the people here do a great job of making it interesting, especially when they chose to display photos of my old bands in a recent 'Pub Rock' exhibition.

Welcome to the ACT!

As I write this, I'm actually in a car parked in Canberra, the Australian capital. Why? I've got a permit to be here for a few hours on a family mission i.e. helping daughter move house. But I'm not legally allowed to get out of the car, which will be soon laden with a young woman's possessions. I do want to get right inside this story, but as much as I feel at home in a car, it's getting hot. You can probably guess the date. It's early 2021. The coronavirus has made some of Australia's more ridiculous borders very real. But let's travel back to a time, when this city was brand new and 'corona' wasn't even an imported beer.

Sometimes, there's nothing else to do but to hang around your front driveway. In 1970, Canberra, the freshly-built national capital of Australia, was full of them. Although Federation occurred in 1901 and Canberra's foundation stone was laid in 1913, people didn't really flock

We did have our own family cameras at the ready. Here is our driveway, 63 Gilmore Cres, Garran.[9] ACT Margaret, Greg, Stephen, Denis Appel + one of the many dachshunds that fell victim to that nearby road.

to the place. There were still only 15,000 people living there in 1947. But there was a combustion fueled invention that helped get the capital to 100,000 people by 1967. Just around the time my family arrived.

This city was designed for cars, full of brand new roundabouts and empty looking suburbs. Just waiting for something to happen. Driveways were doorways to the unknown. Roads that could lead anywhere. Life was full of possibility. I was seven, and just coming into that age when people could make an entire documentary series about the social forces that mould a human. Thank goodness there were no earnest British types hanging around with TV cameras.[8]

Let's zoom in for an extreme close up. One sunny day, I was looking down at some ants making their way across the exposed terrain of our concrete curve. I realised I had a power that they didn't. Suddenly, I was filled with a bloodthirsty lust. I exterminated all before me. Ten minutes later, I was filled with a hideous guilt. This never really went away. Since then, I've gone out of my way to save ants. I think on balance I have now helped the species more than I've hindered them.

Ants were to play a small part in my life – just about as big as they were in relation to me. Despite their size, they are a species that are always present on the periphery of consciousness. Let's face it. They are everywhere. Especially in this harsh brown land. They don't look like they are going to suffer from environmental change. In fact, they might be all that is left.

Where am I going with all this? Hang on there a moment. I'm transported back again in time to a small caravan on the

8   The British documentary series *7 Up*, of course.
9   Please don't send your feedback to this address, no Appels live here anymore.

NSW South Coast in summer. Caravans are like tiny houses except a lot cheaper, and you can attach them to the back of your car and take them all over the place.

It's inside one that I'm having lunch with my cousin Frank, and some kindly old friends of the family, Kit and Les. Must be the early 'seventies now. Maybe I'm ten. They serve up something with tinned corn on the formica table inside this small hot metal box. With the tantalising sound of the surf so close, it isn't hard to imagine ant surfboards. So I tell them all about my concept. Perhaps an ant could use a piece of corn for pleasure? Ant surfboards. The yellow plastic 'belly boards' that were common surf craft for kids at that time, may have been the inspiration.

Maybe my companions think I'm a little weird, but it makes for spirited conversation during our caravan lunch. After all, Kit and Les were artistic types of the old-fashioned variety. Les did watercolours of nature with the odd human element like a boat or a caravan, and both him and Kit were in a symphony orchestra.

Now dear reader,[10] it's not a strong anecdote, but what I'm trying to illustrate here, is the world I grew up in. It's the old Australia. Because not only could it be a sunburnt land. It could be really boring. We are all born somewhere, randomly, just like any ant. I was lucky enough to be born a middle-class human in Australia in the 1960s. Sometimes, boring is good. My motivation for making up this ant surfboard concept, was to make it less so. And perhaps that's what's behind all art.[11]

In the 1970s, surfing was big in Australia – even in our Canberra backyard. This was a good way for me to get amongst it without the danger of being pounded against rocks, etc. I must have been planning a bit of a pre-Photoshop collage thing with a photo of a wave. Another attempt at making suburbia interesting.

Steve Kilbey, the Church: The one good thing about Canberra is, it's so fucking boring.

Steve Kilbey is someone else who also grew up in the city. I got to know him later in life when he performed in my whacky musical *Van Park* about a bunch of old rockers forced into budget accommodation, in the twenty-first century. His band, the Church, were born in Sydney, but he took inspiration from the dull surrounds of the A.C.T.

Steve Kilbey: Growing up there it was really hot and dry and conservative. Everyone was in the public service. The Bohemians left really early and went to Sydney. I hung around too long. I didn't have many friends and I turned inwards and concentrated on music. If I had been in Sydney, I'd have been chasing girls and taking drugs.

---

10 From now on, let's just assume you are 'dear' to me, reader and I'll use this phrase more sparingly than in *Confessions of a Lighthouse Keeper*.

11 Or is it sex? Although surely sex is about making the world less boring. So, same thing.

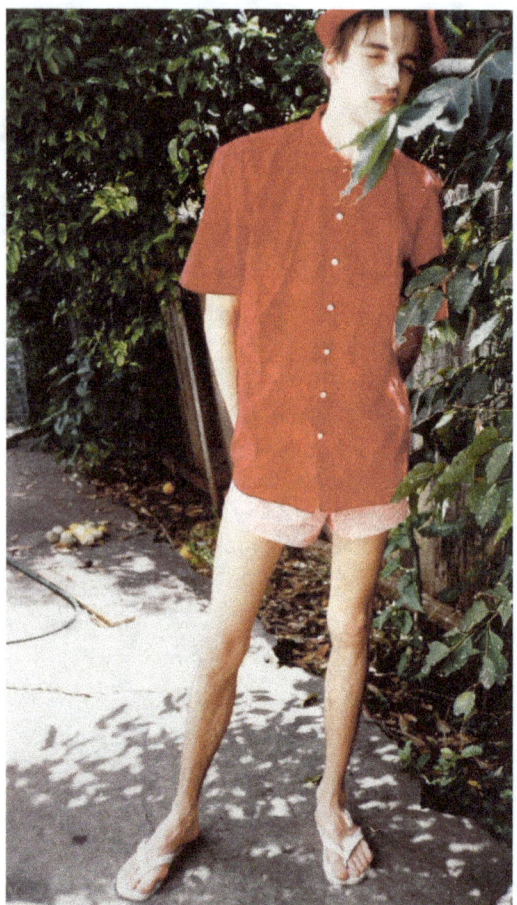

King Ben.

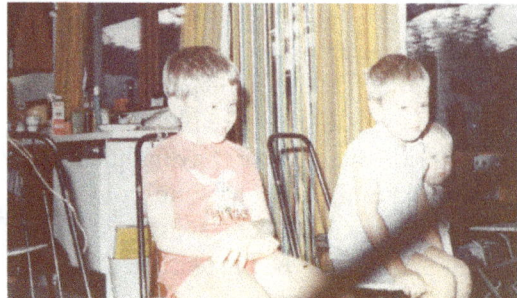

Television!

Widdershins.[12] 'He knows the cities coast to coast, working for Australia Post.' His post office funded life was so boring, that he started to take notes of all the insects in the backyard, including ants. It was a fascinating piece of documentation and I was most impressed with his scientific sampling. To this day, he has taken his work to the highest office in the land. He writes Hansard for federal Parliament, a fastidious written record of every word spoken in the chamber by our elected leaders. The architecture of the Parliament House building in Canberra does have a touch of the ant nest about it. Ant nest combined with roundabout.

Steve would eventually go to Sydney and do all these things. Becoming a Rock Star. Living the dream. Hitting the road.

And now another ant story takes me to Sydney in the mid-'eighties, where I was living my own modified version of the rock dream in an inner city band with a small following. Juliet, the singer and my girlfriend, also from Canberra, had led the way. With me following swiftly.

Another ex-Canberran, our friend Ben, Sting's mate, was living in a group house we all frequented. I tried to capture his personality in one of my songs 'King Ben' by the

Children, back in those ancient times – the 'seventies and 'eighties, we had no smart phones, no internet. What did we do with all that time you spend staring at screens nowadays? It was this spare time that allowed us to really get into the nature that was all around us. This is the evidence I bring to you from my memory of these distant times.

12 This was the band I formed with Juliet Ward, once our best known band, the Lighthouse Keepers, had imploded. For whatever reason, they enjoyed an even more modest success.

The driveway gets more crowded as time goes on.

But maybe we were just waiting for smart phones to happen? We did have television, a kind of crude early version of these personal screens. And that was very exciting for us. In Canberra, we had three whole channels. Out of this big, cumbersome device came some exotic creatures to colour our world.[13] Adam and the Ants, for example. In 1980, they came out of grey British punk, put on some colourful outfits and makeup, and tapped into a whole micro universe that we all knew on a deep level. They did tap a lot too, with those two drummers. Enough Ants. Let's move on.

We certainly got out of the house a lot more than children seem to these days. Our parents didn't seem to care where we went that much. We roamed free. Crossing roads wasn't seen as a task that required any adult supervision. In fact, roads were an important part of our world. We rode bikes, skateboarded and generally felt at home on the tar. The smell of hot tar on a summer's day still brings back memories of a distant hazy world. And that world all began at the driveway.

And so my old driveway in Canberra, will be the starting point for our new journey. Because I feel the text contained in this work may be best read like a map. An old-fashioned folded paper one. We are going places together, it's something of a road trip and a mind trip at the same time. Most of the time, we will follow time forward – the traditional way. But occasionally we will be forced to detour. Of course, life is a journey in itself. But we will stop – we will go to different towns, visit different characters and see what we find.

I remember a promotional campaign that captivated me back then. Shell passports. In the early 'seventies, Shell petrol stations issued passports that you could

---

13 Colour TV didn't come to Australia till 1974. America had it in 1954!

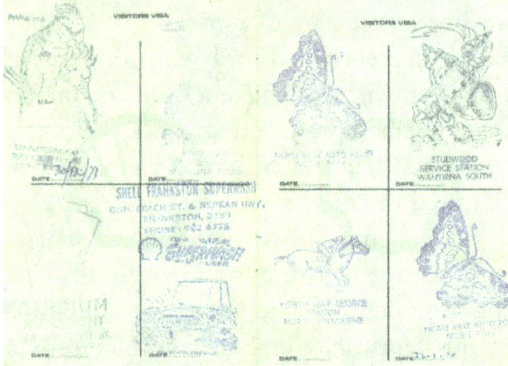

get stamped at any Shell petrol station you stopped at. Dad, dutifully got them stamped everywhere we went. Does that sound like a boring land? Those were the days when someone came outside and put petrol into your car for you.

And if there was something wrong with your car, that same person might even be able to fix it right there at the petrol station! It's probably wrong on some level to be nostalgic for petrol stations. But they were something else then. Monuments to Australia's collective obsession with road trips. An obsession directly imported from the USA.

Australia is in an interesting location as far as world culture goes. Let's face it, the culture I grew up in was basically a cross between British and American – with America firmly in the front windscreen as Britain began to flash past on the side. Multiculturalism and Indigenous rights were only just beginning to flicker into view on the horizon.

Let's investigate Canberra a little further, before we get out of the place. My first band Guthugga Pipeline, which got together in 1979, were part of a small Canberran subculture that for some reason looked to a working class English movement for inspiration. It got mixed up somewhere along the way. There was a gaggle of punk bands around in this very insular scene. Like the Vacant Lot, the Young Docteurs, Tactics, Thalidomide, the Liquidator, the Framed and Myxo.[14]

[14] Just a few others include the Word, the Vitos E, Msfits, Club Of Rome, Quintrex Bop, the Chancres, the Royal Family, Fab, Moral Majority, Manshead, the Creeps, Capital Punishment, the Plunderers, Steve Grieve and the Mourners, Duck, No Concept, Tidal Wave, Falling Joys, Secret Seven, Hell Yes, Armoured Angel, Adrenalin, Real Gone Lovers, the Pheromones, the Naturals, Gadflys, Horrorshow, Texas Massacre, No Remorse, Skin Disorder, the Degenerates, Carkillers, the Reaction, Slab, Young Men Going Places, Naughty Rhythms, Liquidator, the Investigators, F-troop, No Quarter, Black Rose, the Professionals, Urban Chaos, the Jones', Crow, the Juju Men, Choix, the Same, Human Zoo, Grinder, the Untouchables, Kates Birthday, Daddys Coming Home, the Crack, Village Idiots, Ssdc, Four Thousand Million, Apparent Death, Bladder Spasms, Ska-trek, the Latenotes.

Steve Kilbey: I remember when Canberra had its first proper punk night in 1977. It left a big impression on me. The main band were Myxo. The lead singer came out with really long hair and a beard. That was a no no for punks. He had cockroaches for earrings and he walked out on stage and went 'you fucking hippies!' He was about as punk as Mary Poppins.

It was indeed a confused version of punk. This weird antipodean version of punk was common to most cities around the nation. It is remembered fondly by more people than seemed to be in any of the audiences at the time. To get a feel for a small scene within a small scene, let's look back at the written evidence from the national capital. You may have noticed the Guthugga Pipeline Press house that publishes this book. The name has also been used for a record label, when the Lighthouse Keepers put out the original hand drawn cover version of the single 'Gargoyle' in 1983. But it is an ancient name, going back to our first band in Canberra in 1979. It goes back even further, as it is misspelling of an actual pipeline in the Snowy Mountains scheme. I guess you could call Guthugga Pipeline punk… sort of.

Gavin 'Gus' Butler, Guthugga Pipeline's singer: We didn't have any ambition whatsoever, beyond just getting up and having a play. You read about scenes, which are really competitive. But there was nothing competitive about that scene, because there was nothing to compete for.

Our teenage mate 'Scaley' posing with car.[15]

The main attraction was probably the easy chords and 'any one can do it' aspect. This is what I wrote – in the early 1980s – when I was around twenty – it combines my new experiences in a musical gang with writing techniques from somewhere over the rainbow. The same place that ant surfboards come from. Let's begin this journey with some florid prose.

15 'Scaley' was derived from Andrew's surname 'Fish'. He was also called 'Git' for some reason. He was not a punk, but seemed to deal with it, like many of our disparate group of friends in the late 'seventies. I have heard from another source who knew him later on, that things didn't work out that well for him, which is not good, but here he is looking happy and flash with a car. He must have just got his licence. The world was waiting for him to drive through it.

Guthugga Pipeline, 1978. Photo: 'pling

A SAFARI IN MUSIC

THE GUTHUGGA PIPELINE STORY
by Greg Appel

The moon sets over the desert dunes of the wild desolate Sahara, a child cries in Southern India. A Russian voice said something unintelligible and was answered in the same strange dialect. In Scotland, a person slept, then woke for a minute, then went back to sleep. A small furry animal scuttled across the dark empty highway in Canada, near Hudson Bay.

But in the other hemisphere of the world it was day. The sun went down on all the land masses of the south, huge countries that had been colonised by Europeans in the last few centuries. Here new cultures, formed by mixing other ways of life, were beginning to emerge. Forces of light and dark were mingling with cultures of wide open spaces. Channelled into the metropolises. The intoxicating rhythms of the south were being fused with the textured melodies of the north.

It was in this daylight section of the revolving orb, that three minds were wandering around in bodies in close vicinity to each other. It was amongst this joining of the cultures that three hands shook to become the basis for the phenomena that was to be called 'Guthugga Pipeline'. The hands belonged to Gavin Butler, Stephen O'Neil and Greg Appel. We shall henceforth dispense with their rather ridiculous real names and enter the surrealistic world of their abbreviated names. 'Gus', 'Hairy' and 'Ap' respectively.

The 1977 explosion of youth awareness, branded by the manipulating fingers of the media, 'punk rock' travelled towards Australia on a camel train, and about two years later, the filtered scorched and thirsty version arrived in Canberra A.C.T.,

Australia, which would later be called the city of punk by some people. It was this movement that brought together the minds and bodies of Guthugga Pipeline which they used as a stepping stone of evil. We shall now also dispense with the term 'punk rock' and also 'new wave' as the lads would like and explore the band as the individual entity they were so much.

'Hey, Hairy. How about bringing your guitar over to my house to practice?'

'Okay Gus' said Hairy, in his limited vocabulary that had been condensed by living in a small hamlet outside of Canberra, called Uriarra, for so long.

A drummer, or stick player as one of the members jested, was thought essential after the band had practiced a few times. Graham Steadaan was he. So the lineup for the notorious 'Carpo's' party was established, Gus singing, as his musical talents were rather limited at this stage of his life, though he would later prove himself able on a number of instruments. 'Gray' on drums, Hairy and Ap alternating on bass and electric guitar. Some of the songs they performed that first glorious night were 'Anarchy in the UK!' (sometimes A.C.T. was substituted for U.K.) also 'Love Comes in Spurts', 'No Fun' and some originals, 'Flowerpot' and 'The Dream'. The rest is history.

I shall not go into their rise to prominence. The new 16-year-old wonder drummer Wayne Miller or the bass players of personality Jack Woodrow and Nick Ketley are by now household names. Pages and pages have been written on Guthugga Pipeline. The twenty or so places they played at, the incidents, the tensions and the end with the gradual dispersion of members to different walks of life. But

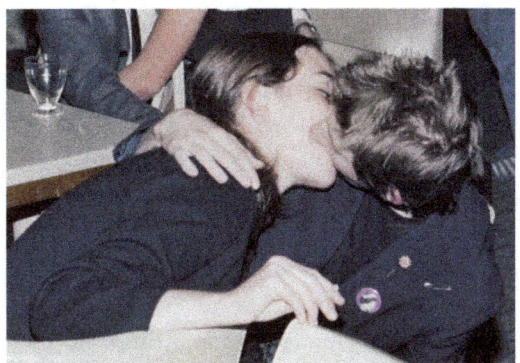

A rare moment captured by legendary Canberra photographer 'pling: Gus gets lucky at a Guthugga Pipeline show!

still today they have music in their hearts. They have been analysed and reanalysed. I will just say this, that if they hadn't been, things mightn't have been. That is, that if the group had never formed a whole chain of events could have affected the world and everything we know in it. If they hadn't played that certain night, if that person hadn't lingered that little while longer to hear their last notes, if that person couldn't get up in time to catch his plane to America, if the plane he was catching lingered for just one minute waiting for him, and if that plane missed the Russian fighter carrying a load of hydrogen bombs by one minute, then what could have happened? Many games like this can be played and even someone from the most distant province of China could trace themselves back to Guthugga Pipeline. However, this is pointless, and we can only thank them for saving us.

Let us take a different footpath trod by few. I will lead you into the area of their persona – and that way give you some interesting insights into the questions that surround them.

Let us start with 'Hairy', born one morning in about 1961 in a hospital somewhere in Australia, a cry is heard that is the echo of the future, his guitar virtuoso. Little information is available on Hairy's early life, and we can only speculate on the pair of eyes looking around, seeing buildings and vegetation and the familiar faces of his family, the hand clenching at the air as if trying to rip something.

The information on 'Gus' is a little more in depth and my research in the libraries of the world led me to a little cul-de-sac, called quaintly 'Harper Place'. It was here at number 24 that Gavin lived his life out. He had a succession of pets. Some dogs and some cats. From an early age he was a bit of a rebel and his white stringy hair was a bit longer than the other little boys' mums would let them grow it. But the rebelliousness only made him more endearing to the people around him and he rose to the pinnacle of dux of Garran Primary School. After this, the change to high school brought dissatisfaction with the education system and eventually with the world that would strongly be reflected in his songs for Guthugga Pipeline.

A little scenario from his life may give us a glimpse of his soul. We catch him in someone's backyard, the evening sun is beginning to sink and the trees cast long shadows on the lawn. There is a slight chill in the air and steam comes out of their mouths as they wrestle and grapple in a seemingly pointless manner up and down the yard. There is an egg-shaped object they appear to be vying for possession of. They are playing football, the score is 368 to 341.

The other little boy comes into focus, his name 'Ap'. I will let you into another secret, this little one is me. There is little I can say about my young life, except that I was a sensitive and humorous figure, with a hint or tragedy.

The other members of the band form a subgroup in contrast with the three core members. If it could be drawn, I would draw a small triangle with the three core members' names at each apex and an outer diamond with the names Jack, Nick, Wayne and Graham in respectively smaller letters. However, I feel this geometrical representation has its limitations and does not give the entire three-dimensional story of the conflicts and consensus between these humans brought together under the banner Guthugga Pipeline. A tiny flash of this outer diamond can be seen by looking further than lines and spaces.

Jack, a social chameleon with a certain beauty and charm, wielding his bass as a weapon against the values and personas that society was forcing upon him; Nick, a newspaper delivery boy who acted as a sponge absorbing others and moulding them into a new distinct personality. Wayne, filling the songs with glorious crescendos of drum solos and, finally, Graham mellowing out the beat with subdued rhythms.

It would take trees of paper, nations of forests to go into every single detail of Guthugga Pipeline. Every word spoken, every thought, every action in each person. However, I hope that I have given you a glimpse through the keyhole into infinity. I will finish with a list of ventures that the Pipeline has emptied into, Manic Rhythm, the Human Salamanders, the Grant Brothers, Tex Truck and the Semis, the Particles, the Lighthouse Keepers and host of others that I don't know the names of...

So, this long short story leads us to the point that Hairy joined myself and Juliet Ward in the Lighthouse Keepers and we plied our rinkety musical trade from Sydney to Europe 1983–86. But I've done that book. If you are reading this and for some unlikely reason have not read *Confessions of a Lighthouse Keeper*, think seriously about reading it. It will help. In this work, I'm trying to keep a good thing going and fill in some of the cracks that appear in that work. Or maybe I'm trying to inflate some empty spaces! We won't know 'til we get to the end.

Much has happened since I wrote that book. Fires, plague and mad world leaders. Where was James Bond when you actually needed him?[16] Politics has become colourful in a scary way.

Tanya Plibersek MP, a Lighthouse Keeper fan who kindly wrote the intro to *Confessions of a Lighthouse Keeper*, has been the federal Labor member for the seat of Sydney, in the relatively sane nation of Australia. She has worked in the national capital since 1998. She knows Canberra well. Or does she?

Tanya Plibersek, ALP MP: I'm the last person really to ask about what it's like to live in Canberra, because when I'm there for work, when Parliament's sitting, the hours are just so unfriendly to do anything beyond working.

When I grew up there in the 'seventies, Canberra had just one Parliament House now known as Old Parliament House. A long white building with vast surrounding grounds, where things unknown to us went on. My main memories of it often involve pulling up nearby in a car at night. Friends would vomit into the convenient shrubbery that seemed to be everywhere and perfect for the occasion. We had not learned how to hold our grog.

Eddy Jokovich, New Politics: The Old Parliament House was a much smaller place. Because it was much smaller, the interaction between politicians was more convivial. So, even though they were at loggerheads on a day-to-day basis, they still passed each other in the corridors and they'd mingle more often. There's no solid research about this – it's more hearsay from different politicians who traversed the Old Parliament House and new Parliament House – but they say the old House ended up developing more solid legislation, better outcomes.

The new Parliament House was opened with much fanfare during the 1988 bicentennial. It's much bigger, like a giant hobbit house that you can get lost in. Politicians from opposing parties don't run into each other naturally. They can also escape the press easily, via a bat tunnel. They only do 'doorstops' when they have their press grabs all nice and ready for public consumption.

For whatever reason, the neoliberals that inhabit it, have become a lot more rabid than their predecessors. Malcolm Fraser, a much hated liberal leader from my time in Canberra, now seems to be remembered like a kindly old lefty. Are we drifting further to the right all the time and therefore causing this rear vision effect? Or is it just a distorted form of nostalgia?

---

16 Yes. James Bond is licensed to kill. There was a problem President in the US from 2017 to 2021. Drop him in the White House via helicopter or big drone!

Tanya Plibersek: You look at someone like Tony Abbott, who really made a career out of being completely uncompromising. He even voted against things that he previously advocated, because he was never going to give any ground. I think that really divisive, no holds barred, campaigning, has been a definite negative. There was a time when seeking, something that broadly most people could live with, would win you points. Now it seems like the best way to make your case is to smash your opponents and make it impossible for them, to do anything. Even if they are elected government of the day.

Most of us who grew up in the capital were oblivious to any politics going on. The Canberra that I grew up in, was the capital of a land that was trying to come to terms with itself. Its real history was whitewashed at school and made extremely dull. It was all about gold rushes and explorers. We still sang 'God Save the Queen', but without much conviction. I think it would get a more resounding performance from Australians today. Weird, but probably true, based on nothing but speculation. Though I have noticed Australia Day has become a lot more subdued. Maybe it's a country that still wonders what the bloody hell it is.

Tanya Plibersek: Being patriotic doesn't mean being nationalistic, or thinking that you're better than other countries, it just means like a deep and abiding love of your country. You can have an inclusive patriotism that fights for better or you can have that awful nationalism that we see in some other places. I think this time is a really huge potential inflection point in Australian history, where we say — What worked for us during COVID-19? Our universal health system worked for us, we saw the value of permanent jobs with decent pay, where people could take time off if they were sick. I think that it is right to compare this period to after World War Two, or the depression.

Indeed, all around the world we've suddenly been forced to live in our countries of birth — love it or not. They have become very real. As we journey it might be the time for us to think about what it means to be Australian. Does it mean anything in this globalised world? It's interesting to think about what was going on so close to me in Canberra during this period. In that Old Parliament House. There was an Australian brand forged that was much clearer than it is now. You could tell by the type of politicians that got voted in. Bob Hawke seemed like the ultimate Australian.

Eddy Jokovich: Hawke was a bit of everything. He was born in South Australia. He grew up in Western Australia, during the time he started off in the union movement. When he became a politician in 1980, he actually represented Victoria. Then he died in New South Wales. So he's sort of been all over the place. But, as you would know, all roads lead to Canberra.

Bob Hawke has become a mythic figure for Australians of a certain age and in the wider world. He even makes it into UK dramas like *The Crown*, where he appears as a super 'ocker', semi moron, who snarls some unlikely lines about getting rid of the Queen. Gradually, information has filtered down to us about his 'lifestyle' back in those days, it doesn't seem to make him any less loved. Politicians and their entourages seem to treat Canberra as a twilight zone. Journalists had a code with their politician drinking mates that seemed very similar to the musician's one. What goes on the road, stays on the road. What would the Hawke era look like if everyone could see just about everything he did and comment on it, in real time?

> **Eddy Jokovich:** Bob Hawke was a womaniser – there's no secret about that. That's probably one of his few negative parts. But I think the main thing is that he wasn't a hypocrite about it. So we have had recent issues with politicians sleeping with their staff and that sort of thing, but on the other side of that, publicly preaching family values, the ones they never follow for themselves. Bob Hawke never did that sort of stuff.

If I thought about his personal life at all at the time, I might have thought Bob Hawke was married to Hazel and had a couple of kids and seemed to cry a lot. He was part yobbo and part new age man. He didn't seem to drink once he became Prime Minister, although it was a legendary part of his past. He had a long-standing beer drinking record at Oxford University that the nation was privately stoked about. A few TV crews over the years have told me that he might have had the odd can of beer in private at the Lodge, when he was supposed to be teetotal. But the information is foggy. Strangely, this same period when I was most involved with the music scene, the 'eighties, was also a time when a craze for Australiana took off around the globe. For a few flute-infused years, Paul Hogan, Greg Norman, Olivia

Crocodile Dundee, 1986.

Newton-John and the rest of the gang made merry to the sound of Men at Work. Hawkie was right in there with them.[17]

Maybe the Crocodile Dundee incarnation of Australia was part of a nations' crude attempts at identity. Somehow, its innocence found a global audience. Inner city Australians were cringing as Paul Hogan pulled out a large knife to send a New York mugger scurrying away clutching his much smaller knife. But you couldn't say it wasn't popular. However, this international craze faded quickly. No one remembers Koala Blue.[18] Australia is back to its former place in the global consciousness. Barely there. Just the way we like it.

17 I have been involved with numerous montages of this kind in my documentary work. Ergh!
18 Olivia Newton-John's Australian-themed international chain of fashion stores.

DRIVE TIME: AUSTRALIAN ROAD GUIDE | GREG APPEL

Hawkie could get away with wearing 'budgie smugglers' in the 'seventies and 'eighties, no worries. In 2014, Tony Abbott could not. But a new generation in Canberra are reclaiming the look – Simon Kragh and friends in 2021.

But hang on everybody... get in the period car of your choice and ignore seat belts. Let's get out of Canberra for a start. Nice place but I wouldn't want to get stuck there for too long. It's also notoriously difficult to find your way out of. Every road seems to loop back on itself. I still get lost there and I learned to drive in it's empty suburbs. The original designer of Canberra, Walter Burley Griffin and his wife Marion were rumoured to be into the occult and put all sorts of symbols into the layout back in the early nineteenth century. Making it full of circles. Perhaps that's where the problem started. You can enter, but you can never leave.

Gus Butler: I remember going to Belconnen Mall at night, when I was in my early 20s and just being basically alone in this concrete and glass structure. It was like being on the set of a science fiction film.

But let's turn on that handy modern device we all have ready to connect. How about a bit of music. A soundtrack to our journey. What would a road trip be without one? There is of course an accompanying podcast where you can hear some of these people say some of these things for real in beautifully mixed stereo. Appropriate music? Can I start with the music that reminds me of

Canberra. It's not so much British punk, but what came before it. I spent a lot of time listening to Elton John when I was young. I got the amazing double album of *Yellow Brick Road* one Christmas. Like millions around the world. First track – mind blowing. Very appropriate to Canberra, with the sound of wind and not a word from Elton for a long time, some chords on the organ, then some kind of early synth thing. Perfect, because Canberra definitely has its spooky side. As we head out of town, and the dexterous band enters, let's reflect on the year that album came out, 1973. We catch a glimpse of Bob Hawke and an unnamed woman going into the Rex Hotel. We see his wife Hazel sitting in the lodge watching a steamy scene on TV; it's *Number 96*.

And so we leave the Australian Capital Territory. Capitals, borders, states have never been under such scrutiny since Federation. COVID threw a spanner in the works. Who would have thought those arbitrary borders would mean so much. Australia is a divided country again. There's been positives in the crisis, but there's also been a lot of border shutting and posturing. Suddenly, people know their state leaders. Who knows what will happen by the time you read this? Hopefully we are all free to go where the road takes us.

As we drive we will gaze back through time via the places we visit. Sound like fun? Traipsing around the country in un-airconditioned vehicles was how I was brought up. And I can't say I didn't enjoy it. Occasionally car sick, occasionally needing a piss but ashamed to call a halt to a never-ending drive. Otherwise, these are happy memories. As they would be for many travellers. Australia in the second half of the nineteenth century seemed to be all about holidays. It's what we lived for, and seemed to be the basis of our civilisation. The whole 'lifestyle' concept may have been hatched in the old parliament house back in Canberra around the time I grew up. If it did, it would definitely have been in the notorious non-members bar. Where journos and politicians got loose with each other, in a way that is no longer acceptable.

I imagine Bob Hawke (in his ACTU days) knocking back quite a few schooners with the unruly mob, deciding lifestyle was part of the Constitution. John Howard was obviously listening as he would occasionally make oblique references to 'our lifestyle' in the future as PM. And 'ScoMo' is a like an extra from a 'seventies Australian film like *Don's Party*. Maybe hanging round the pool with a beer.

We're heading out towards Yass on the Barton Highway, a nondescript but pleasant enough drive, skirting the massive sprawl of houses that make Canberra the capital of a suburban nation.

Goodbye sweet childhood.

THE VEHICLE: INSIDE THE BUBBLE

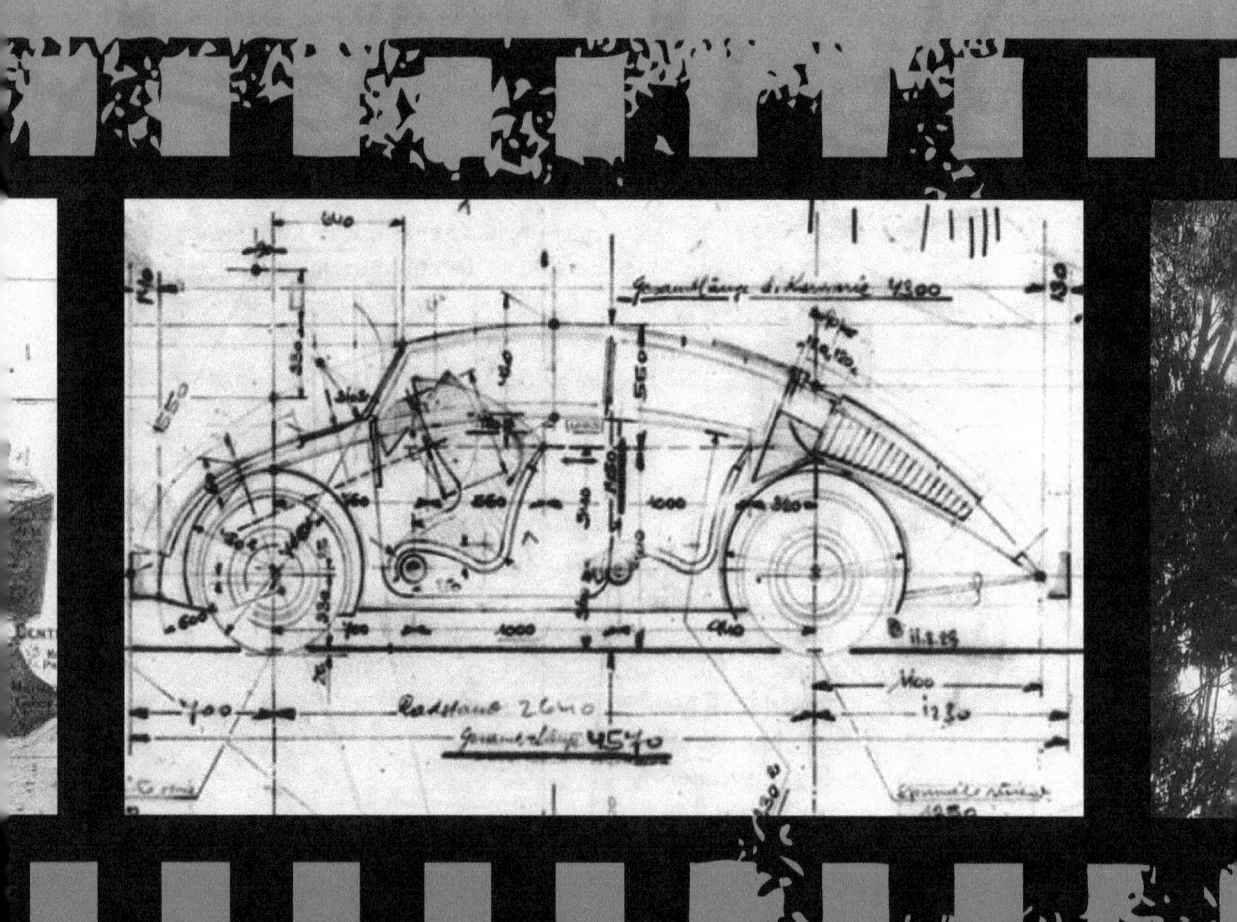

MUSIC
* *Road Runner*, the Modern Lovers
* *I Want to Do it With You*, John Paul Young
* *You*, Marcia Hines
* *The Road to Gundagai*, Jack O'Hagan
* *Family Man*, King Curly
* *Close to You*, Carpenters

DRIVE
Recommended – Kia Cerato; also the Toyota Prius hybrid, which has quietly become a great vehicle for Australia's lack of electric vehicle infrastructure if you are looking to cut down on fossil fuels.

EAT
Good road food? Very difficult to find. Many years ago, I proposed an outlet to be known as Grizzler, based on vegetarian/fussy eater diets. I've often travelled with these people and it's really difficult to feed them. Then Olivers appeared, exactly according to my business idea. Another money-making idea I never followed through with. Am I recommending Olivers? It serves a purpose but could do without the magical new age branding.

VISIT
Your inner self. It's little known that extended periods of staring ahead at highways can achieve the same state as Sotāpanna Buddhist meditation.

It's inside the car that it all happens. For a scarily large part of my life, it's been a home. When I think about time spent awake, there's quite a lot of it inside a moving vehicle. I've always commuted long distances and worked in such a way that I was endlessly driven. Not by ambition, but by my own driving. In fact, my first job in TV was as a driver.

In the 'eighties, when I first worked for the ABC, I had to get a Commonwealth drivers licence. I don't think I had to do anything but fill out a form or ten. But at the time, I did have a talent for reverse angle parking. I remember a group of people cheering one particularly difficult performance. But enough boasting.[19]

The interior of a car is where it gets interesting. It's an intense space. It can be a psychologist's couch, a family court or a *boudoir* in the most French way. Many use these confined spaces for good old fashioned sex. I remember a long northern NSW journey with a girlfriend on a rainy night when the car interior seemed to be all these things. It alternated between music, laughter, shouting, tears and sex, all the way from Sydney to Nambucca Heads. The rain pelted down as it can do on the North Coast. We did at least pull off the highway occasionally. Happy days.

As I interviewed people from far and wide for this project, I found these dramatic moments were common. Some of the interviews came from fairly close to home. Like Sam Wild from down the road. Her first car was a '67 Valiant Safari station wagon purchased in the 1990s. It was a useful escape mechanism.

---

19 Today, this is called 'self promoting' and seems to be a good thing.

The white stallion.

Sam Wild, arts mogul, Bulli: Getting in the car and escaping for an evening because I'm angry about something. Getting in the car and just driving. And then the mobile starts buzzing and they're starting to say exactly what you want them to. Where are you? Come back home, come on, stop doing this. And you're just driving and you choose to drive. And that mobility, the ability to get in the car and leave and then choose to come back – is probably the loveliness about a car.

From a scientific perspective, the car itself can be part of the 'extended self'.[20] As we use this complex tool to navigate the even more complex world we live in, it becomes part of us. We feel the speed humps, we take an aggressive tailgater very personally, we jam on the brakes. People seem to change personalities inside this protective bubble. It's like social media behaviour in the non-internet world. It can certainly be part of how we define ourselves. Sadly for me, I am now defined by a small red Kia. Once it was a sleek white Holden HK, known somewhat ironically as 'the white stallion'. It had a tiny but thick, fur covered steering wheel and a spider encased in the gearstick knob.[21]

One of the questions commonly prompted for users in the never-ending log-ins we have to navigate online is, 'what was your first car?' This is because it obviously sticks in people's minds, along with their first pet (which is much more fuzzy). It's often functional and second hand. Is there not a place in driving history for this humble vehicle that has taken a person from A-to-B fairly reliably but is not an expensive or highly modified throbbing beast? Brad Owen is a motor enthusiast and the museum coordinator at the National Motor Racing Museum at Mount Panorama in Bathurst.

Brad Owen: There are motor racers who drive like grandma on the road, because they get their satisfaction from driving on the track. But whether there's

---

20 I read it somewhere, probably *New Scientist*.

21 I don't believe any insects were harmed in the manufacture of this knob.

Then there are special vehicles built for sex. Myself and Paul Clarke taking my brothers panel van for a 'writing weekend' in the early 'nineties. No sex involved.

a space for the very conservative driver who's worried more about the number of cupholders and how many speakers the stereos got, that's probably not us. But there are certainly a lot of other motoring museums that are more general who look at that. Because that's all part of the evolution of the car.

As young adults, these vehicles are our first homes. Mobile, unhygienic and prone to accidents. My own was the classic VW bug. An off-white 1962 model. So, the same age as me. We all know these cars had something to do with Hitler and had motors in the back. They had a particular sound that is still occasionally heard from those retro Kombi vans that now sell for a fortune.

Today, the VW Kombi van is a nebulous signifier of 'sixties 'freedom' and attracts the mature crowd who go by the unattractive labels 'baby boomer' or 'grey nomad'. For me, the VW Beetle took me out of Canberra and into the wider world. In relative comfort, and often seclusion. It was there I was able to listen to music, if the sound waves could rise above the engine noise, or just sit in quiet inner contemplation. Is this not the state that meditators seek to embrace? Easily achievable via a long car journey. Road trips are also about breaking down barriers.

Brad Owen: Maybe it's the stereotypical bloke thing, that you don't talk about your feelings. But I think when you're sitting in the car, and you're both looking at the windscreen, you can have conversations that you might not be able to have face to face, because you're not making eye contact.

I'm not prone to rhapsodising about cars, so I won't. But in one of those strange twists in life, I got to know a VW specialist very well. He used to own a garage on Broadway, across from Sydney University. He sees the car as a living being.

Tom McCabe, VW specialist: You could see the car as a body. And blood being the oil. The engine, the heartbeat. And there's blood pressure and fuel pressure and oil pressure. And yes, they love to breathe and exhaust air like we do.

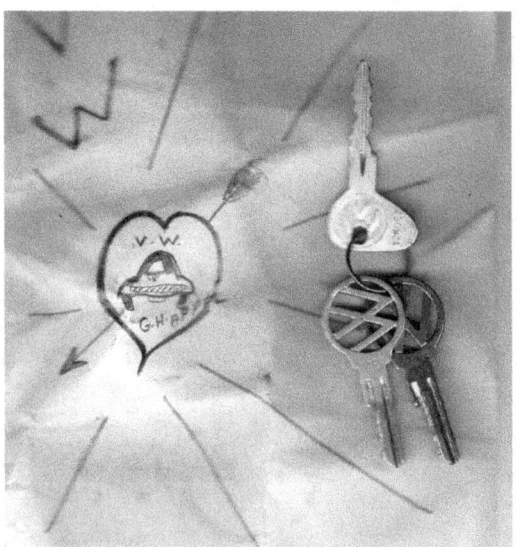

It's amazing – I've kept my first set of car keys, and more amazing that I found them!

A real life flashback! Amanda Peacock as a child with family, funsters and bus.

Tom has often advised me on cars and has been unceasingly accurate in his choices. The modern equivalent of the VW bug is the Kia or Hyundai. Both of which I have possessed. He tells me they are made by factories next door to each other in South Korea. I hope by the end of this writing, I have the electric version of the Kia. They can't be too far away from my price range. It's pretty boring spending a lot of money on a car, and can be pretty boring to read about, eh? So let's keep 'moving forward' as they say in corporate jargon. This is all about the journey, not the vehicle.

Someone who has been beside me on many of the journeys we are about to undertake is Amanda, my partner for want of a better word. We got together in the twilight zone of inner city Sydney in the 'eighties. Somehow, we managed to escape its darkly gravitational pull and have produced two grown children – who seem relatively well adjusted.

Very broadly speaking, we both work in the arts, sometimes together. Both of the children seem averse to working in the arts, we may have gone a little too hard with negative aspects of this glamorous world. Amanda's history is like a parallel yet inverted version of my own upbringing. A true child of the 'sixties, in the re-enactment sense. Unlike me, who was a child of two not very groovy doctors. She grew up in the very small world of Australian musos, jazzers and hippies. A lot of her childhood was spent on the road. Some of it literally, as her old man (as in father), turned a bus into a house. The Peacock family headed off to the Aquarius festival in Nimbin in 1973. Pioneering a lifestyle now called 'van life' on social media.

Amanda now likes her house to remain in the same place, for as long as possible. We agree on this basic principle and have remained relatively fixed for many years.

At this point, I have to come clean about my style of driving. Amanda thinks it's safe but at times sluggish. There's a scene in the now classic *Kath and Kim* TV series, where Kath is being driven somewhere by Bret.

'Can't you go any faster!'

While I'm not suggesting I have been the recipient of such comments, I am also suggesting it is possible to imagine how such a scene might occur. It's a pressure cooker inside the domestic car bubble that couples drive around in.

Then there's also other drivers out on the road that have strong opinions. Occasionally you see into their vehicles and realise why urban traffic is insane, aggressive and unpredictable. These people are not fans of my necessity for a ten-car gap ahead of me. So, they're constantly flashing lights, yelling and cutting in front.

Mind you, I have yet to discover a style of driving where you don't get any flashes, snarls or honks. The same thing happens if you try and become one of them! Indeed, it is a religious experience to drive through a city. A Buddha-like demeanour is the only way to navigate heavy traffic.

There's only one time I truly succumbed to road rage. Me and Amanda had just had our first child, Zelie. She never slept. Except for one place. Strapped up in a baby capsule in a moving car. Late one night, we were both feeling miserable and tired as Zelie looked at us with eager wakeful eyes.[22]

We took her for yet another drive. Probably not at a very quick pace. Behind us, the flashing and shouting began. This time I stopped the car and blocked the agitated

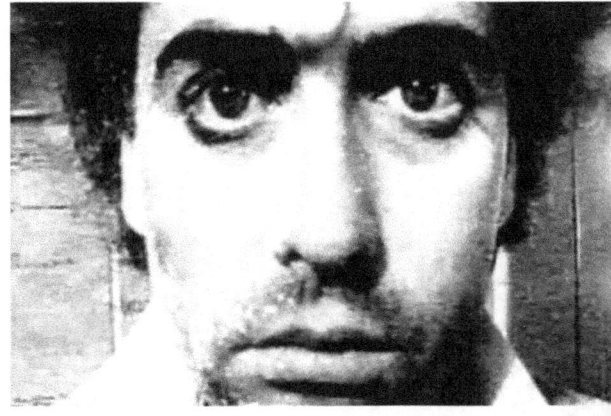

Bottle man.

driver. I was so tired and angry I got out and went towards them. I was wearing a long coat over my pajamas, giving me an ominous aura.

I was very lucky that the other driver was a frightened looking young woman. I got back in the car and decided to never do that again if I could possibly help it.

We had our first child around the time *Bottle Man: The Movie* was created – and I looked something like this.

On another occasion, not far away, I saw a man pull a metal jack from under his car seat and go at someone who'd upset him in the traffic. I didn't want to find myself face-to-face with one of those people. So as we journey, let's try and remember that other drivers are an unknown species. They could have had difficult lives. Their own babies might never sleep. But I know that *you* are a good person, otherwise you wouldn't be reading this.

But we all know people who change personalities once they're behind the wheel.

Frances Green, producer, Melbourne:
What are you saying here Greg? I know my driving style is assertive. And I reckon

---

22 At the time of writing, this same creature (now in her mid-twenties) jumped into our car and told me of a night seeing a band in Sydney that will be easy to date. The last COVID restrictions on dancing in NSW were lifted. She told me that the crowd moved awkwardly until something just clicked, they went berserk, jumping about everywhere! 'this is what it's like to be human!' Sadly, I am going to have to keep updating this footnote. As I write, we're back in a long lockdown.

Frances Green and Lancelot Sello on the road in Namibia, 1996.

that comes from driving overseas, in particular bigger cities. It probably can be construed as aggressive. But I remember a friend of mine from Johannesburg, seeing me drive, would say 'you are a true Joburg driver.' And I wear that as a badge of honour.[23]

Even though they might change characters in this driving bubble, the pleasure of travel is surely in the people. It's about new experiences and unexpected moments. A dull freeway might just be our starting point and also our saviour. The road has a mystique that never seems to be dulled by its dullness. The myth seems to easily incorporate long hours spent staring ahead in a rumbling enclosed space. It's about the wide horizon, big skies and something so ethereal that it can't be clearly spelled out. Everywhere and nowhere at once. As we set off, let us reflect on how we got to this place. Via the USA of course! It all started on Route 66. A highway where you could get your kicks. Really?

Route 66 doesn't really exist anymore except in song and mythology, it's been bypassed all over the place. Though plenty of *kitsch* signage and tourist traps remain. And so as we travel across our own country (which at the time of writing is all we are allowed to do) perhaps we can speculate on why Australia isn't America?[24] Indeed, we are thankful for this at present. I remember listening in to a conversation on a long flight (in the days we could freely fly in and out of the country). It was someone who came from the Indian subcontinent talking about the country beneath us. We were flying over central Australia. It went something like 'where are all the people?' It seemed in comparison to India, Australia was very underpopulated in similar geographic regions. It caused me to wonder why this was so.

I must say, I personally don't mind it just the way it is. But in America – our totally culturally dominating mad uncle – it also appears more populated right across the country. If you look at the election map, it's full of red in that middle part. It seems like it's home to a reasonable portion of the seventy-four million Trump voters. Australia has more of a marginal climate in the interior, and much less people, but maybe something else is going on?

I set out to speak to someone with more knowledge on the subject than me. Ivan Coates lectured at Sydney University on modern American History. So as part of my informal research, I pointed a record-

---

23 I made a documentary in South Africa with Frances Green, *The Team that Never Played*, about pre-apartheid football.

24 Although I am writing from an Australian perspective, may I welcome any international travellers who have joined us.

One of Australia's car operas – set in the fictional town of Paris, Australia.

ing device at him. I began by asking, was there any room now for Australia to take up the slack that America now seemed to be offering the world? Could we become a superpower? It's a big question and Ivan did his best to reply.

Ivan Coates, reluctant academic: We have to think about what it means to be a superpower. Globally strong, with political, military, economic and cultural powers. It's pretty hard to see on a comparative basis, Australia being able to match the predominant countries on any of those levels.

But why did America become a superpower in the first place?

Ivan Coates: There's two parts to it. There's the ever growing economic might. Then there's global circumstances. The opportunity to step forward and turn economic strength into being an actual agenda setter on the world stage. The two world wars really weakened the European empires. America didn't have all that. They just kept growing economically. America is a big country with rich natural resources. But they had to be exploited. So I guess you've got slavery coming into that as a major leg up. You've got imperialism of various sorts. Even after the Civil War, the American interior was still not strongly occupied by European settlers. It was after the arrival of trains that the whole interior started to be heavily settled. Some historians would see that as internal imperialism. Taking over all that land, effectively by force. Then there's immigration. Bringing in all the people that can settle that land and exploit it. Industrialisation really hits America after the Civil War, and you get the growth of the first corporations. Massive wealth is accruing at that time. Then external imperialism as America starts to look for new markets. Part of being a superpower is the soft power as well, exporting that cultural dominance.

Hollywood was the machine that pumped out American soft power. An amazing phenomena that has mesmerised the world. It created mythologies about the USA that are so persuasive, it's very hard to write about the subject with a clear mind. It's an integral part of our collective id. In that respect, I guess we are all born in the USA. There seemed to be just the right mix of population, intellects and fairy dust to make the city at the end of Route 66 go off sometime in the early twentieth century.

The Hollywood machine fed on all sorts of things, even niche movements like beat poetry and beatniks. It was the car that took the beat poet ideals out of railway boxcars and onto the road. Followed by countless films, books and songs that mythologised the endless black, snaking American highways. Like much of our post-war culture, Australian car design was directly lifted from America. There must have been a time, when all a budding Aussie business mind had to do was take a trip to California, observe, copy and return to Australia. Then paste. Insert house, car, fashion, etc. Wait for the money to roll in.

Clinton Walker, writer: Australia is the second great car country after America. Australia did it best after the Americans when we got *Mad Max* and all that. *The Cars That Ate Paris*. I call them car operas. Cars taking over a small country town. I don't think there's anything too complex about the metaphor. Which is simply that the road is going to take you somewhere else.

Ivan Coates: America was also a huge centre of auto production, and Australia just never came anywhere near that. It's pretty hard for Holden to really make its mark on the world with the internal population we've got. But, with the mythology of internal travel, you can see the comparisons. We've got that big space, and people can drive through it. They are quite similar experiences. But, if you look at the Australian outback, we think of it in very mundane terms. Yet the American outback is suffused with this mythic kind of layer through films, music and books. The car was also seen as part of the American quest for rootless journeying. The lone male in search of freedom, often from the 'stultifying' ties of domesticity. It was that right of a free individual to do as they please. Australia hasn't really taken that libertarian idea on board quite so strongly. We have more of an English background, an idea of the fair go, of unionism.

It would seem that the American myth of cars and freedom is built on an ability to turn something inherently boring into an almost religious experience. It's quite a talent. America seemed to have the perfect population in both numbers to sell cars and culture to, and a general zest for life. The Australia that I grew up in was still very British and uptight, and that made a difference.

Ivan Coates: Britain was still a strong Empire at the end of World War II, but it was really brought down soon afterwards by decolonisation and political and economic problems. So that really left America to step forward if it wanted to. And it did. Russia and the whole Cold War thing probably helped them as well, because it meant the world had to choose between one of the two. Australia's just not in that kind of position.

I think many Australians would join me in feeling lucky not to be in the position America finds itself. In some ways, it's great to be an invisible continent as far as the rest of the world is concerned.

But there's a part of Australia, especially the one I grew up in, that has been largely invisible to the Europeans that live here. Indigenous Australians have been here all along. John Paul Young, the Scottish born, 'seventies pop star is perhaps not the first person you would think about to comment on this. However, during a long rambling conversation in the middle of the recent epidemic he told me this.

> **John Paul Young:** The real treasure of this country is our Indigenous people. It really is an untapped wealth of information that we have really yet to get onto. And we've got to start, we've got to start involving Indigenous people more in what goes on in this great land. They know more than we will ever know. And, unfortunately, our presence has destroyed a lot of what they knew. But it's not too late if we think in this way. I really believe that it should be grabbed with both hands. That sort of stuff is the real meat of this country and it should be explored. It's just so sad that the dollar rules everything. Hopefully, this coronavirus thing might have woken some people to the importance of things other than just making money.

Travelling around the country, it's impossible to ignore the past. Over my lifespan this world has become more visible. In my work,[25] I've filmed small parts of a wider Indigenous renaissance in art and culture. But as you will find, the story of the people that originally inhabited this continent keeps appearing round bends in the road. It was there all along and we are all part of this larger story – for better or worse.

John Paul Young became well known in Australia as the guy who sang 'Love is in the Air' and punched Molly Meldrum. He

was also a major star in South Africa and Germany, but that's a whole other story. John is also a keen car enthusiast, who has roamed around Australia since he left his job as a sheet metal worker in the Sydney suburb of Liverpool. He played in venues all across the nation in the wild 1970s. But John never saw that much of the towns he played in, because he was always working or partying – hard.

> **John Paul Young:** I remember Cairns when there was not a brick. The whole of Cairns was made of timber when I first went there in 1975. But I've seen a lot more of this country in the last thirty years doing the Variety Bashes,[26] because I'm not driving. I'm sitting in the passenger seat.

---

25 Largely due to Amanda's work in the Aboriginal and Torres Strait arts area.

26 An annual cross country charity drive.

Zelie Appel with Dog and Tucker Box.

If we are thinking about what it means to be Australian, John is perhaps the most Australian a Scott can be. When he came to Australia as an eleven-year-old child, he was greeted off the boat when he first docked at Perth by a mysterious man. He took John to nearby Kings Park and plucked one of the huge gum leaves from the trees that abound there. He told John to crush it, saying 'this is the smell of Australia'.

John Paul Young: It's such a wonderful thing for that guy to have done that. It was his regular thing he used to do whenever a ship came in there.

What a way for future Australian royalty to arrive in this nation. John was eventually crowned King of Pop in 1978. John thought it was the 'kiss of death' for his career. And, indeed, his hits largely dried up afterwards. It was the last year that this ceremony was held in Australia. But it also means John Paul Young is still the reigning King and Marcia Hines the Queen of Pop. What do they need a constitutional referendum for? It's all sorted.

How the hell did we get to John Paul Young and Marcia Hines? It was the road. The long and not very winding road that goes all round Australia. Time to listen to some 'seventies pop and forget about today. My favourite songs from both these artists contain 'you' in the title. 'I Want To Do It With You' – John (and producer/songwriters Vanda and Young) at his peak. And plain old 'You' by Marcia. So, turn on the imaginary radio and slide that red thing over to 2SM, settle back and enjoy – yes, you.

And so we're heading down the Hume Highway into the rolling hills around Jugiong and Gundagai. If wind farms can be both ominous and spectacular, these ones are. Looming up behind steep hills. These hills can be brown or green depending on the rainfall. They look ancient.

Off to the side of the highway, the small dog on the tuckerbox is a restrained version of the big things that we will flash past our windscreens on our wanderings. It's a fairly average looking rendition of a fictional dog in bronze, four miles away from the true fictional location. In the famous song by Jack O'Hagan from a whole century ago, the dog sits on the tuckerbox – nine miles from Gundagai. This statue was put in a spot more convenient to the petrol stations and highway. Come on Australia! How will we ever cut it internationally with that sort of soft diplomacy.

WHAT GOES ON THE ROAD STAYS ON THE ROAD: TARCUTTA

WIRADJURI COUNTRY

MUSIC
* *Time*, Pink Floyd
* *Cicada Cycle*, Tarcutta (the band) an obscure experimental outfit from Melbourne.

STAY
Halfway Motor Inn Tarcutta. I can't say this is recommended as I have not stayed there. However, it has the ambience of a 'seventies motel, and one of its positives is listed online as 'Halfway between Melbourne and Sydney'. Or, alternatively, Mates Gully at 38 Morrow Street in nearby Wagga is really nice if you aren't searching for 'seventies motel ambience.

EAT
At this point in your journey, maybe just some fresh fruit may be good. Alternatively, 'The Ten Mile Holbrook' at nearby Holbrook (sorry Tarcutta) can be partially recommended. A man told us the sausage rolls were 'to die for' and they were, indeed, very good.

VISIT
Tarcutta Op Shop – some great 'seventies crockery, etc.

RANDOM POINT OF INTEREST
Before 2011, trucks roared up and down the Hume Highway which was 'til then, the main street. It's bypassed now but you can still look at them in the giant truck car park near the middle of town.

Out there in the wider world, where they make cars and all sorts of things, modern tourism has pretty much removed anything of pleasure from the very process that created it. You only have to look at what has happened to Venice and Paris. Mobs of people come from all over the globe to get exactly the same pictures of the Mona Lisa or continue squashing St Marks beneath the water.[27] It's a totally unsatisfying consumer experience that seems to be unstoppable.

I think the best way to have our little driving holiday is to do the opposite. Australia itself is a good place to start, the rest of the world barely knows we're here. *Terra Australis Incognita*, it remains. So we've got a head start. Let's look for any high rated tourist icon and head away from it. Five stars; bad. Maybe we find the lowest rated and most uninteresting places possible. Or

---

27 Coronavirus most likely just a blip in the action.

even better, we could go about fifty kilometres away from the highly rated place and still benefit from some of the star power. I think Tarcutta in NSW may be high on this list. It should have been the national capital.

We have already visited the real national capital. Canberra sits uneasily and at an incorrect distance between the two big cities of Australia. The location of the national capital was meant to be a compromise between Melbourne and Sydney. This was from an earlier time when the states bickered about borders and the like. Federation had not yet forced the nation to join as one. Canberra was not even on the Hume Highway that now joins these two cities. But Tarcutta is, and not far away is the highly rated town of Holbrook.

As we drive, turning up the volume on the entire album of Pink Floyd's *Dark Side of the Moon*, I think it's worth settling into the Hume as a place in itself. Because we are somewhere, even though we are moving forward and swaying rhythmically in the car seat. It seems strange to think that before it was a road, there were competitions in the early nineteenth century to set the land speed record between Sydney and Melbourne on this route.

Rickety looking cars used to belt up and down paddocks and dirt tracks, bringing this road into being. And, of course, before then, there were tracks Indigenous people used. Like many present day roads, they follow at least some of these ancient routes. This highway supposedly follows the route that the white explorers Hume and Hovell made from Sydney to the Victorian coast. But who knows whether it does? Regardless, it was named the Hume Highway in 1928. It's Australia's three-and-a-half star highway, part of route number 1 that goes around this massive continent. The Hume's double-laned freeway is a fairly straight line between the country's two most populous cities. It's got a lot straighter over the years. There was a time when the Hume Highway was a far deadlier place. Enough to have an 'eighties band name themselves the Deadly Hume.

Blak Douglas: Ordinarily I sit within the 'allowed' ten-kilometre-over-the-speed-limit within NSW. A mixture of 'flirting with danger' and 'because I can'. It's not the case in other states however: for example, Queensland, where they'll nab you for a couple of K's over and sneakily set up speed cameras in ordinary tradie utes. Regarding 'top speed'... I'll flatten the pedal any chance I get on a gun barrel highway in a remote area.

I have spent a reasonable amount of time in cramped conditions inside vans with fellow band members, plying our trade around the country (and Europe a little). The most common route I found myself travelling was the Hume Highway. As we ate our toasted ham and cheese sandwiches, washed down by VB (almost fash-

ionable back then) I often wondered about the towns we passed through. And over the years, these thoughts kept coming back. What sort of person would choose to live in one of these anonymous towns in the middle of nowhere?

Tarcutta is not a place many people would think of visiting for tourism purposes. The nearby town of Holbrook has the monopoly on everything tickety boo (arts and crafts, jams and frilly curtains, etc) and someone even plonked a submarine in the middle of town – drawing tourists like a magnet. Why? It's one of those unknowable factors that make the road a mystical place. So, most people would go to Holbrook if they really wanted a stopover in the middle of their trip from Sydney to Melbourne.

To test my theory that non-tourist locations can actually provide a more satisfying travelling experience, let's randomly stop at Tarcutta and see if there is anything of interest. My memories of this town were from the days when it signalled the halfway point on a much longer, more dangerous journey on the Hume Highway. Today it's been bypassed by a double-laned freeway. But Tarcutta is still there just a short loop away. I must say it seemed a lot nicer than I remembered, now the traffic has largely gone. There's some nice old buildings and a pleasantly ghostly feel to the town. At the time I stopped, there had been plenty of rain and the Riverina area was undergoing a bit of a green and leafy renaissance.

A few people very politely dodged my request to interview them, and usually pointed me to someone else over the road. Faye Belling, who volunteered in the Tarcutta Op Shop kindly obliged. I told her that I found the town very tranquil without all the traffic.

Faye Belling: You get used to noise and traffic. I live eight K's out and pretty close to the main highway. But I notice the road when it's quiet, I sort of hear the silence.

Faye had been in Tarcutta since she was born there in 1951. She was born on a farm and became a farmer's wife. A solid community member. She just loves Tarcutta. So much so that she was awarded an Order of Australia medal, for service to the Tarcutta community.

It wasn't long before I was sitting down with another Tarcutta lover. In a nearby café, Alan Podmore kindly shouted me a coffee, as well as answering my impertinent questions. He was the most well preserved 77-year-old I had seen in quite a while.

Alan Podmore: It must be in the water we drink. Grew up here, went to school here and have done a lot of business here. It's always been a very countrified place and a very friendly town.

It turned out Alan was a stock and station agent and had done a bit of time as a cattle auctioneer, which he demonstrated to me in a style that would win any slam poetry contest. He was struggling to think of anything bad in his happy life in the country. His most fond memories were of the Tarcutta rugby league team. When they were in winning form.

Alan Podmore: The only negatives were when we'd play football or cricket and get beaten. Nobody enjoyed that. It was always great to win. But we had some very, very good sportsmen out of Tarcutta. Tony Roche, who was one of our great tennis players.

Alan was a good talker and took me through the town's history as he had witnessed it. Happy times in a country town. Any trouble makers were rounded up by the police and made to play rugby league. Some of them became star players for Alan's beloved Tarcutta team. Alan talked about gypsies passing through town. I had never heard of gypsies in Australia.

Alan Podmore: They used to have big fancy flashy cars, and they'd have those bauble things in the windows...fair dinkum they'd pinch the eye out of a needle if they got a chance.

But they were never able to make Tarcutta part of their circuit, because 'the big Sarge would fix them up'. Today, Tarcutta is just one of many towns in the Riverina area that seem to be doing pretty well. I learned that it was not so long ago that farmers were only making $300 an acre (apparently not good). But during my visit, due to good rain and good prices, it was now $3,000 an acre (very good). Kids were staying on at farms and coronavirus escapees had added to the mix. It was now that much better to be in a town in the middle of nowhere in a country far far away.

Trucks have been central to the town's economy, and unlike gypsies, truckies were well loved. There was a flood in the 'sixties that saw 500 truckers being fed by the town

gily groups of musicians coming through town when it was on the main highway. He certainly did. I thought he was going to put them in the gypsy category. But again, nothing but great times as they stopped in at the monthly balls, in order to check out the local bands.

Alan: The bands would stop in, have a listen, have a drink, have a bit more to drink.

Now the Tarcutta story takes a turn. Because, perhaps foolishly, I turned to the internet for inspiration. What would you know? There was a band called Tarcutta, they had a YouTube clip up and it only took a few messages and a trip to Melbourne and we were sitting down to talk music and location.

Justin Buckley, Tarcutta (the band): I guess we're proudly one of the country's least successful bands.

There are two Justins in this band of three. It turned out Justin Buckley had grown up in Tarcutta along with his bandmate Justin Wheelan. They were articulate and funny. But the band's music had yet to find a mass audience.

It could be described as light industrial and features Justin Wheelan's Hammond organ pulsating through various speaker cabinets, accompanied by drums and guitar and a bit of this and that. Justin Buckley was nostalgic about his country childhood in Tarcutta.

for a week. And the town remains a truck drivers mecca to this day. Many choose to live in Tarcutta, because of its central location. There's even a truckies memorial in the middle of town, where a very well attended annual event is held every year. It's a reminder that the Hume remains deadly. Although it was a lot worse back in the old days.

Alan: The road was probably 12-foot wide and rough as bags. There was countless accidents with narrow bridges. Trucks were a pretty rough mode of transport then.

I asked Alan if he remembered any scrag-

BAD ROADS COST LIVES

Unrelated but so related. We all had one of these ads on the wall in the 'seventies. Evoking that ultimate road trip we aspired to.

Justin Buckley: I don't know if I'd bring my children up there, but certainly for me there was plenty of it that was great.

Some of the band's music evokes this rural childhood. Cicada noises, drums that sound like sprinklers and wistful chords that evoke Pink Floyd. Justin had tickets to the 1987 Pink Floyd concert in Melbourne, but his mum wouldn't let him go. Hence, a life devoted to the trippy instrumental form that his favourite English band made their own (there are long bits where Pink Floyd sing, of course). Listening to *Dark Side of the Moon* now as we drive, do we wonder if the world will ever be able to sit still through an entire concept album of such magnificent ambition again? It's like super muzak. But deservedly popular, the masses got that one right.

Back to the road. Tarcutta is a town with a name that evokes road work for me. With tar in it and cutting sort of in it. It sounds like some sort of high-vis worker that you might zoom past on a drizzly night, feeling better about your own line of work. But of course, that's not right. Like so many Australian towns, it's an Aboriginal word. Justin told me how the hard core locals pronounced the word when he was growing up. It sounded a lot different. More like 'Tarcudda', and it now made sense that it could mean 'meal made from grass seeds'.

Justin Buckley: It was certainly not something we discussed at school. No one ever really talked about the origins of the name when I was growing up.

Place names often carry a deeper history than the people of today can remember. Who would have thought the name Tarcutta, would be so evocative of a future road building material? Tar would be laid down the whole distance of the road, by the end of the 1940s. The symbolic end of the deadly Hume era would have to be the Tarcutta bypass in 2011. A couple of years later, the whole road became a dual carriageway. Boring.

The tar-rich Hume Highway has been part of Australian musical history since it was sealed and even before. Those first rockers, like Johnny O'Keefe and Col Joye and their bands, imitated the craze from the USA, and just like their American idols, they would soon be saying 'What goes on the road, stays on the road' to each other. It got louder into the 'seventies and 'eighties. The early Australian rockers were also frequently in car accidents. It really was the deadly Hume then.

Having worked on quite a few music documentaries, I've heard numerous road stories from musicians that probably should have stayed on the road. It can be a sexy place in moments, but it can also be incredibly boring.

Rock writer, Stuart Coupe, was a band manager back in the 1980s. He took Paul Kelly and the Hoodoo Gurus across Australia and America – the spiritual home of 'the road'.

> **Stuart Coupe:** We were on the road. Yes, there was alcohol. Yes, there were drugs. Yes, there were girls. Yes, there was silly behavior. But a lot of the behaviour that really happens on the road is just mindless fun because everyone gets incredibly bored. You're spending a crazy amount of time in hotels. You're spending a crazy amount of time on tour buses going up and down highways or in airports. And after a while, as Paul Kelly sings, every fucking city looks the same. I spent many years traveling the world, people say, what was San Diego like? I say 'I don't know'. We arrived in darkness. We left in darkness. I could vaguely remember what the parking lot of the venue was like. Bus surfing – it descends to that level. You're so bored that everybody fills up a coffee cup or a glass full of booze and then attempts to navigate their way from one end of the tour bus to the other end at 150 kilometres an hour. Hysterical fun. But it actually seems like one hell of a lot of fun at the time. Would you do it any other time in your life? Probably not.

In the same period Stuart was stuck on buses with boys (some girls) and drugs and booze, I was going across Australia with the Lighthouse Keepers playing country towns. These could be fun times or not, depending on whether you could give the crowd what they wanted. As a band, we were fairly oblivious to their needs and favoured our original material mixed with a few eclectic pop and country classics.

> **Juliet Ward, the Lighthouse Keepers:** We'd play three half-hour sets in a town that had never heard of us and were wondering when we were going to do the Jimmy Barnes cover. In between half-hour sets, there'd be a half-hour break. They'd put the jukebox on and everybody in the audience would get up and dance. And then when we got back on, they'd all sit down and audibly groan when we came back on stage. Those shows were really hard.

Juliet Ward on the road, 1984.

you get up with a morning hangover, like a badge of honour. The drug thing wasn't major in that era. I mean, people were taking speed and popping some pills and doing stuff, all that, but it was more alcohol based. And it was pretty intense. I remember standing beside Ted Mulry, one day on a bus trip around Australia, having a slash against the wheel of the bus, and we're pissing blood. We looked at one another, and I thought, maybe it's time we pulled up just a little bit...

But there was another road-based job which was all about making money – the travelling salesman. These characters roamed the nation's roads in the middle of the last century. They seem to have disappeared now. In fact, disappearing was a common male characteristic back then. Something that is increasingly difficult to do. The travelling salesman made a profession of it. Rock writer Clinton Walker knows the type well. His father was a travelling salesman.

Then there are the people that work in that profession that is actually named in honour of the road. Howard Freeman began working as a roadie in the 1970s when Australian rock 'n' roll was in it's adolescence. I interviewed him for a Radio National program in 2004.

Clinton Walker: I had a pretty middling relationship with my father for a lot of reasons. That's just what he was. To be a travelling salesman, you had to be a garrulous guy. He was the life of the party kind of guy, told all the jokes, and was sort of good looking. There would always be jokes in cheesecake magazines about travelling salesmen. They had a barmaid in every town. And as far as I can tell, that was my father's reality. There's a family legend that we had a sister in Shepperton. I don't really care.

Howard Freeman: It was basically boys town. There were no limits. There was no preset code of behaviour. When you went on the road in those days, you were treated like a bunch of rebel bikers. People didn't want to have you in their hotels. So the places you stayed in usually weren't first class and they were sneering at you. You worked your ass off. Your downtime was limited. If you finished work at two in the morning, you had to be up at six. You'd put in a day of fun and laughter in two hours. You'd drink double, so you wouldn't have to walk back to the bar as many times. You do it tough and

These travelling salesmen just might take their barmaid friends to a nearby motel for some of the fringe benefits of the job. Sex

Howard Freeman: The bands had an image of well coiffed, nancy boys. You go into country towns and you could walk down the street and get a smack in the mouth. I've walked through the streets in outback Queensland where guys have walked up to Daryl Braithwaite and hit him about the head, just because he was there you know? Because their attitude was, you were something they could never be. You're coming into their town, you're ripping off their chicks. Because all their girlfriends would ever talk about was the band. Yeah, we've had moments where people have driven around our hotels firing shots in the air trying to get us out of town, throwing bricks at the bus, firing arrows at me, been jumped on, been thrown about.

Today, a musician might not get shot at but there is a different sort of weapon that has changed the wandering minstrels world. Steve Kilbey toured Australia and the world with the Church in the 1980s, when communications were a lot more limited.

in highway hotels has a certain allure. A night spent with trucks passing back and forth in a montage of Doppler sound, can be arousing. It might also be an opportunity for us to take a quick stop and investigate the subject. Where would motels be without sex? They'd be horrible noisy uncomfortable rooms. And lonely ones at that. A truck passes in the corner of our mind with some noisy brake screeching for added effect. Musicians are also travelling salespeople of a kind. Howard Freeman, the roadie from the 'seventies, knows well the creed of the road. 'What goes on the road stays on the road.'

Steve Kilbey, the Church: The sex part is a lot more dangerous now because you've got Facebook. There's that saying, 'what goes on the road stays on Facebook'. There wasn't social media in those days. I remember soon after I joined Facebook, there was a friend of mine who was in quite a big American band. He had had a few nights with a young lady in America, and then, as they might have said in the Middle Ages, he cast her off discourteously. And she made sure that everybody on Facebook knew that he, this man, had a very small whatnot. And that's the kind of thing we didn't have. There wasn't that in the 'eighties. I guess one could be cast off discourteously and have no recourse.

Steve Kilbey as Nebauchadnezzar – a mystical prog rocker character from the 'seventies. Part of the eclectic cast of my musical *Van Park*. About the end of the road for some old musos.

But the road isn't just full of male rockers on medieval quests. Women are equally driven to this mythic road. Australian roads have a personality all of their own. Because it's such a large country, with a spread out population. There are roads that can barely be called roads.

Sam Wild, 2021: It seems that my experience of driving has always been through rough tracks, taking the dirt track, and going through the bush, and trees and things like that, rather than that sense of driving for miles on open, near stark landscapes where you casually come across a scary sort of motel or coming across the petrol station where there's a cranky man at the counter. I think it is different in Australia, but it's still a unique experience travelling in a car with your stuff in the back and looking for somewhere to stay or planning to crash in the back of the car and not worrying too much.

And out beyond Tarcutta, the road gets a bit more interesting. Dear driver, we're now going to get off that double-laned freeway and head cross country. The white bones of a dead tree and sharp cold air tell us that the landscape is changing. After all, we're listening to *Dark Side of the Moon*, full of soundscapes – and all about madness. It was another roadie, Chris Adamson, working for Pink Floyd, who recorded the spoken lines that set the album's tone in the track 'Speak to Me'.

> I've been mad for fucking years,
> absolutely years,
> Been over the edge for yonks,
> Been working me buns off for bands.

The road can be a strange place. My fellow drivers, we are taking the scenic route from Tarcutta, via Snowy Mountains Highway B72. We turn off it just before Cooma and head to Jindabyne. We've exited because we take a quick detour to Guthega Dam, where we pay homage to Guthega Pipeline (you remember the misspelled Canberra punk band from earlier) it brings water that provides hydroelectricity to the nearby Guthega power station. It's very near to the NSW ski fields Blue Cow, Smiggins Holes and Perisher, where I was fortunate enough to spend some time in my privileged youth. But I think Guthega

The real Guthega Pipeline. What a beauty!

was lodged in my young mind when I went on an excursion to see the Snowy Mountains Hydro Electric scheme in sixth class. We stayed overnight at Jindabyne and I remember some dark thing happening that meant we were all confined in our rooms. The singer of Guthugga Pipeline, Gavin 'Gus' Butler would have been on that same excursion. Drink, drugs and sexual awakenings were all starting to happen. Mr Mallet wouldn't have any of it on his watch. He was an ex-army alcoholic headmaster, let loose on an innocent primary school. We cowered in our frigid grey rooms. At least I did, I was terrified of authority. Still am. It's the Australian way. Gus was probably loving it.

On with the journey. After Jindabyne,

Snowy Mountains Highway B72.

we go crazy with the small mountain roads winding back and forth from Victoria to NSW, the C608 to Wulgulmerang, the C611 to Bonang, the C612 to Lords Hill/Bomballa and the B23 to Caan River... and then the A1 Coastal Highway (part of Highway 1) and, finally, the C617 to Mallacoota. During border closures, this area must have seen plenty of illegal farmer action crossing back and forth between the states. It is quite the drive for Australian mountain scenery.

There's a mysterious drowned forest feel to it at certain points with the occasional misty dam. Built in the days when dams were about nation-building. Things to be admired. Whatever the foggy history, it's well worthy of a four-point-five star rating for the countryside, perhaps not the speed. But we will leave this sort of stuff to the NRMA magazine and concentrate on our mission. People, history and a deeper understanding of ourselves. I mean that in

Gus from Guthugga Pipeline before he went 'punk'.

the most global sense – you non-Australian travellers.

MAURICE STREET, MALLACOOTA

BIDAWAL COUNTRY

MUSIC
* *Golden Miles*, Healing Force
* *Share This Wine*, Things of Stone and Wood
* *Dishwashing Liquid*, the Widdershins

STAY
Silver Bream Motel, a classic atmospheric motel near the middle of town, but beware of spooky dreams.

EAT
Café 64, not bad for straightforward takeaway fare.

VISIT
The Bunker Museum – a little out of town, you get to go down a reversioned World War II bunker. They've got a nice collection of bits and pieces. Some Japanese midget submariner's shoes for example – found on the beach, from the period they operated off the coast here. Japanese subs sunk twenty-two ships off Eastern Australia, all unreported at the time due to wartime censorship.

RANDOM POINT OF INTEREST
Mallacoota became internationally famous for a very short period in the 2019/20 bushfires, surrounded by fire – one road in, one road out. The Navy eventually evacuated the town, for a moment Mallacoota became the third most googled word, read on for the scary story from the people trapped in the town.

In the warm late morning light, a little exhausted by the long drive, it's a very picturesque time to write 'as I write'. Mallacoota, just inside the Victorian border from NSW, seems to be surrounded by water. I'm on a headland looking over an estuary that looks across to hills towards Gabo island and the sea. There's NSW over there. At this point, we're still in the period where you need a pass to go from NSW to Victoria, but at the time of writing there was nobody to check it, and nobody really seems to care.

Earlier we were wondering whether Canberra was established in the right spot. Tarcutta was a possibility, but Mallacoota truly is the location that should have been considered. It's not on the Hume Highway, but it's on Highway 1 that goes right around Australia. Well, that's if you turn off and go twenty-five K's down the Genoa–Mallacoota Road (C617). It's nearly exactly equidistant between Melbourne and Sydney, and one of the most isolated areas of Victoria.

My first trip to Mallacoota was just after the 2019/20 bushfires. It wasn't like I was the only person with journalistic tendencies to make the trip, and at times I did feel like a real journalist. The type that are sent by the local rag to door knock following some horrible tragedy. Being on a mission to make a radio program about the main street for ABC Radio National, I set out with very little planned. Sometimes that's the best way. And often it's my way.[28] This would be one part of a radio series 'Greetings from…', something of an audio riff on the local rag

---

[28] I do actually plan and research to some degree but don't want to give too many trade secrets away.

As I write.

concept.[29] For younger readers, the local rag is a local newspaper, from the time when every town had one – devoted to local news and gossip. On my first day there, I walked up and down the main street, Maurice Avenue, which didn't take very long at all. There was a community arts centre that looked like a good place to start. I walked inside and some friendly ladies, who declined to be interviewed, pointed to a room next door. Inside was a heavily bearded man. He was making his own radio program for the local community station. It seemed to feature a whole lot of acid prog rock with occasional back announcements.

Don, also known as King Don, had been in the town for thirty years after exiting Melbourne's Carlton theatre scene and joining the Mallacoota Arts festival.

He was in his seventies and gave off a bit of a Gandalf vibe, and indeed his email featured the word goblin in it. He kindly agreed to do the first interview while in the middle of a back announcement to the small number of people who were likely to be listening.

Don Ashby: My dog, a few tradies. They seem to like it.

In that first interview he told me that he was 'high functioning autistic' and that he'd watched his house burn down in the recent bushfires. But Mallacoota was getting back to its old self.

Don Ashby: In the middle of winter, you could machine gun down the street, and you wouldn't hit anybody.

---

29 Many years ago, in the mid-nineties of the previous century, an ABC TV editor called Steve Brown came to me with an idea about a program about King Street, Newtown. I owe him a lot for dragging me into this project. The series continues...

Coronavirus made sure that the street was fairly deserted at the time. From Don's phone contacts, and the help of Pierre Forcier, a volunteer at the local bunker museum, I began to learn about the people that lived in this little town when it wasn't full of tourists.

Brett Menke, abalone diver: Everything is virtually on Maurice Avenue. You see everyone, because it's a small street.

Naomi Wilson: If you go down the street, everyone will say hello. I don't think there's one local that doesn't say hello. But I've been here nearly eighty-seven years. So I suppose they think 'that poor old lady'.

When I was in my teens, I had a phase where I read books on permaculture, took an interest in beekeeping and studied mudbrick houses. Mallacoota is where it all happened for real. People came here during the 'seventies and actually built mudbrick houses, made music and seemed to have had a lot of fun. Don Ashby was part of a group of people from Melbourne's fringe theatre scene that migrated here. One of them was Bruce Pascoe, the author of *Dark*

Simon Pickworth and me in our coastal prog rock stage.

Aerial photo, Mallacoota.

Mallacoota seascape – water everywhere!

Emu, the best selling non-fiction book about Indigenous agriculture.

Don Ashby: I knew Bruce way back in the 'eighties. I was the manager of a small theatre in the back streets of Carlton. We ended up sharing a house together because we were both in between relationships and all that kind of thing. And he wrote lots of really, really excellent Australian fiction, and now he's become a bit of a public figure.

Bruce has indeed become a public figure, partly because News Corporation and friends took aim at both *Dark Emu*'s thesis and his Aboriginality. But there was a backlash against this backlash and people bought multiple copies of the book, sending it to the top of the book charts. Not an easy thing to do with non-fiction.

Bruce Pascoe (from *Conversations,* ABC Radio National, 2016): When I was about nine, there was a woman who lived in my street who claimed to know about my Aboriginal family. And I found it a bit upsetting. And I didn't know how to react. She got a bit angry with me, she thought I was snobbing them. You know, I was being called nigger at school? Where did that come from? I had red hair and pale skin. So people seem to know a lot more about my family than I did.

When Bruce was in his late teens, an uncle got him a job working on the fish trucks going between Melbourne and Eden. He told Bruce that there were black sheep in their family and one day he'd introduce him to them.

Bruce Pascoe: And he did introduce me to some men at Lakes Entrance in a fishing boat, who he said were my cousins. By the time I was thirty-two, I had a daughter, who was six by that stage, and beginning to ask questions about the family. And I realised then that she wasn't going to stop asking those questions. And that I owed it to her to find out a little bit more. And it's been all uphill since then.

Bruce is now running a farm near Mallacoota that grows Indigenous grains and employs young Indigenous people. But when I asked Don about the Indigenous history of the area, he hesitated before answering.

Don Ashby: According to Bruce, there was a quite substantial settlement here. And they were cropping and had permanent dwellings and all the rest of it. And they all got kind of bulldozed or whatever they used instead of bulldozers in those days, and basically they went away. I believe there were some substantial massacres around here. I have no evidence at all, except just listening to what older people have said in the past or more like what they haven't said, and how they change the subject a lot, when you mention it. And the Kooris don't seem to want to come here.

His answer hinted at a darker story to Mallacoota than fishing tales and mudbrick poetry. Like everywhere in Australia, history is being revisited and people are dealing with some uncomfortable truths. As I got further into the story and stayed longer in town, unusual elements became apparent and it became a darker piece. But not without light. Around Christmas in 2019, flames lit up the skies around the town.

I listened to the stories from a number of people about these wild fires. Some of them were obviously still traumatised. Mudbrick muso pioneers John and Joyceylen Grunden were huddled on a small boat with a random group of people as the flames surrounded the town.

Joyceylen Grunden: We're down there looking up at this redness growing. And as it got darker, it got brighter and brighter, of course, because we could see it was getting closer.

John Grunden: It was completely black at ten o'clock in the morning. The scariest thing to me was the noise that when the weather system came through it the wind came from all directions and it was savage for a very short time. And during that time, there was this weird wind. If you had to do

Don Ashby.

a soundtrack for a science fiction movie, it would have been really good. The fire created its own weather system.

Don Ashby: The (local) shire had done nothing really. They basically told everybody to go down to the caravan park (full of) gas bottles and just huddle. Which was just appalling and we ended up with about 600 people inside an old sports stadium. The fact that no one was killed was just absolutely amazing. It could have been a holocaust if the wind had not been quite as good and if suddenly nine tankers didn't show up.

It was all over the news at this point, 'Inferno in Paradise' type headlines. Mallacoota became central to the international media feeding frenzy as the rest of the Eastern coast burned. My extended family drove through flames from South Durras, near Batemans Bay and made a pilgrimage to the less firey area where I reside. In the ABC

Mallacoota podcast, you can hear some Danish voices, one of them is my ex-brother-in-law, who remains stubbornly attached to the greater family. He morphed into a Danish news correspondent during the fires and could be heard barking into the phone on our deck, saying alarming things about helicopters and apocalypses in his native tongue. It was a Christmas to remember.

In the burned version of Mallacoota that I visited, green shoots were quickly coming back on black stumps. Nature seemed to love the drama. It was a turning point in the international global climate change debate. But some locals saw the fires differently.

Cec Wilson: It was just a camp fire...

Naomi Wilson: ...it's eighty years since I've seen a bad fire.

Naomi had lived in Mallacoota for eighty-seven years. These comments were forthcoming, despite the fact we were sitting two doors away from some totally incinerated houses. Naomi and her husband Cecil had lived in Mallacoota for their entire seventy-year marriage. Cecil managed to put out the flames that threatened to burn their house down with little effort. According to them anyway. The couple were good for a cup of tea and a chat. They seemed to have the secret of a happy marriage.

Naomi Wilson: We're different religions but we both love a good drink of beer.

Mallacoota society had come a long way since they had to get a special dispensation from the pope so that a Catholic could marry a Protestant. When Cec moved there, there were five families in town. Naomi has lived there her entire life. They both seemed to appreciate the changes that mudbrick migrations had bought and another industry that changed the town. Abalone diving. Indigenous people were onto abalone from way back, but Europeans never caught on. It was Australia's growing relationship with Asia that sent the market crazy. There was abalone fever in Mallacoota when Brett Minke's parents arrived in the 'seventies.

MAURICE STREET, MALLACOOTA

Brett Minke, abalone diver: I was born here in 1975. My dad heard about abalone in Mallacoota being a viable income source, and he loved diving at the time. He thought he'd come down here more for the lifestyle than the income. And that's pretty much how that abalone industry was born. It seemed like a lot of people were having a lot of fun.

Brett told me about growing up in a party atmosphere, abalone diving, and the abalone pearls that his dad developed. But the interview took an unexpected turn when he told me both his parents had been on Malaysian Airlines flight MH17. One of two Malaysian Airlines flights that became infamous within a couple of years of each other. MH17 was shot down by a missile over Ukraine in 2014.

Brett Minke: I was in shock. The whole town was in shock. Everyone reacted very similarly. The backstory to being on the plane, was my dad's seventieth birthday. And we'd been in France to celebrate that with the extended family. So we're all there. And we've had this great celebration and then and they happen to be on that one flight. And I guess luckily, we weren't all on that same flight. Even though it's been six years, it's still very raw.

These dark incidents seemed randomly intertwined. My personal experience of Mallacoota was both beautiful and eerie. I experienced vivid nightmares one night and put it down to being so remote. Then there was the coronavirus. The borders kept opening and shutting as I tried to get there to finish the program. Indeed, it was quite a year to remember.

Brett Minke: I didn't mind coronavirus, being a surfer. We get to go surfing anyway because we could still exercise. The homeschooling was tough. My personal thoughts were that maybe the coronavirus was a good thing because people could take a step back and process the fires. Bushfires, well that's just gonna happen when you live in the bush. But I don't think anyone realised it was going to be that bad.

But every radio documentary has a happy ending. The last time I saw Don, he was working on his house. It was half built and he'd made a nice space in a shed where we had a cup of tea.

Don Ashby: I can say that without the help of some very good friends, the house would not be where it is. Helping each other. That's what gets us through. I sat down the other day. It was the first chair I'd owned since the bushfires. And I thought, I've got somewhere to live. Hey wow! I felt fantastic for days after. I've actually got a chair to sit in and it's my chair, and it's under my roof, in my room. And I looked around and go this is where I live. And it was just extraordinary.

Cue the music. 'Share This Wine' by Things of Stone and Wood. One of the pleasures of making these programs is getting in touch with musicians. Well, to tell the truth, sometimes they can be bitter and cranky. In this case they were neither, a band that I learned was connected to the area. I'd been shown a burned shell of a house next to the Grundens' classic mud brick castle. It was the town joke that the Grunden's house would burn easily in a bushfire. It didn't, but next door was the burnt remains of Justin Brady's. The fires had randomly leapt about leaving some structures standing while incinerating others. Justin's band were happy to let us use their uplifting music for the radio piece. It really suited the story.

And to add my little end story to this chapter. I listened to 'Share This Wine' many times while putting the program together. The very appropriate opening lyrics are:

> From this chair, I see the sun
> Bathe me in shadows of commission flats.

It fitted so well with Don's moment of chair ecstasy. But being a fellow traveller in the arts, I heard the lyrics of the second line a different way.

> From this chair, I see the sun
> Bathe me in shadows of commissioned works.

I had a very personal vision of the singer, who I imagined was a painter as well. He was singing about artworks hanging on the wall. I imagined he'd applied for funding, got an arts grant, hung those commissioned works... a whole scenario that seemed appropriate to life in Mallacoota.[30] But let's move on from this imagined scene. Hop in the car, put on Things of Stone and Wood, and hit the one road out of town.

The route from Mallacoota to Port Kembla takes us inland through Bega and some incredible landscapes, as we head back towards the coast. I'm feeling the urge to get the drone out at every turn. To what end I do not know. This kind of landscape is hard to capture, and it's not really worth it, as at every turn there's something better. There's a lot of musicians I know and have heard of, that have now settled in this region. A slightly old world hippy vibe tinkles through these valleys.

I used to travel through here with Juliet Ward in the old days, when we were a fresh new couple, even before we were Lighthouse Keepers, on our way from Canberra to Bermagui, to tinkle our own guitars. The Brown Mountain route (B 72) that links up with our route North (A2), is one of the best stretches of road in the land according to my personal rating guide. I give it four stars. I cannot but think of cassette tapes, Melbourne Bitter and a dog in the back.

But to tell you the truth, I was driving this route just recently by myself and began deviating from nostalgic music, I put on a very unproduced Australian podcast called 'Spirit Sisters'. Amanda, my partner of many years, had alerted me to it, knowing my interest in near death experiences, or NDE's as they seem to be called now. These incredible and sometimes barely credible tales of Australian ladies going to heaven (and hell at points), meeting Jesus and having their lives set on different courses, proved quite mesmerising. The amateur quality of the audio made it all that more realistic and it created an alternative dimension that I entered. The long drive's mindfulness effect we have noted before, with these words from beyond mortal life and visuals of lush scenery – I was in the zone. God's own indeed.

Sections of this chapter can be heard on the *Earshot* documentary, 'Greetings from Mallacoota', ABC Radio National – abc.net.au/rn

---

30 Now maybe that should have been a footnote to the happy ending. Just like this.

WENTWORTH STREET, PORT KEMBLA

THARAWAL COUNTRY

MUSIC
* *Dirty Old Town*, the Pogues
* *I've Been Everywhere*, Aunty Jack Dapto version and Lucky Starr
* *Things I'd Like to Remember*, King Curly

STAY
Try the Port Kembla Hotel, I haven't stayed in there, but I've played in there – with a scraggily group of people. A great old pub which used to burst out onto the streets in the 'sixties and 'seventies. Today, it struggles but it was run by nice people – last time I dealt with them anyway.

EAT
Servo Food Truck Bar, 6–8 Wentworth Street. 'The Servo' is also a live music venue, built on the bones of a petrol station. Suburban reconstructivist chic. Also Kemblawarra Sandwich, 219 Shellharbour Road (on work days). The foodie crowd may just catch on if you don't hurry!

VISIT
Breakwater Battery Museum, also a café just across from it, with a great view of waves pounding the breakwater when it's happening.

RANDOM POINT OF INTEREST
The Sand Hills between Coomaditchy Lagoon and stunning Port Kembla Beach were mined for a while. The sand was sent to Hawaii! You'd think they'd have enough there.

As we go further north up Highway 1, urbanisation starts to fill in more gaps. The road turns double lane. It's still pretty inspiring but we know there's maybe a city up ahead. Cities have their own human landscapes that are a whole other way of navigating the world, but let's stop for a while on the fringe.

It's funny what you remember people saying to you over time. Because you know that they will most likely have forgotten these things. So did I really remember my older cousin Bruce Wallner, saying that cities were in a permanent state of decay and reconstruction? It's an odd, unremarkable thing to remember. But it's true. And as we drive, we are slowing down at the edge of Sydney, in one of its satellite cities. Wollongong. It's a place I know well, for reasons I cannot go into too deeply. I could have problems with stalkers.

Wollongong has its own satellite city in Port Kembla. It's a great example of decay and reconstruction. Along with a local artsy type, Anne Louise Rentell and I chose this place to make what would become the first in the 'Greetings from…' series, broadcast on ABC Radio National, with an accompanying online video.[31]

---

31 www.abc.net.au/radionational/programs/earshot/wentworth-street-port-kembla/11228828

Wentworth Street, Port Kembla, in its heyday (circa 1940).

Port Kembla, or 'Port' as the locals call it, is a special place to those who grew up here. We found it in a state of semi decay, but with artists beginning to re-colonise the main street. A common phenomenon. In fact, if I could get it together to make an app with artist habitation clusters linked to premonitions of rising real estate values, I would do it. For what reason I'm not sure. It would just add to the horrible cycle that makes property the number one conversation topic for Australians. Yet another amazing business idea not acted upon.

Despite Port's rising value as real estate, there's plenty of characters that live there and don't think about the area in investment terms. Some are long termers, some are visiting 'hooker lookers', and some literally live on the street. Wentworth Street, Port Kembla is one of the few streets left in Australia where prostitution still happens on the actual street, hence the name street worker is quite appropriate. Anne Louise had already interviewed a street worker, who we decided to call Fran for privacy's sake. However, I don't think she would have minded having her real name broadcast. She was happy to talk for the camera. The lapel mic is clearly visible in the close up.

Fran has a little throne that she sits on in the street and has seen good times come and go. At its height the Port Kembla steel works employed over 20,000 men (just about all of them were male) but it began shedding workers in the 1980s and today there are only around 3,000.

Fran: I've been working the streets of Port Kembla, oh goodness, for about maybe fifteen years. A lot of cleavage was shown back then, but that's fine. There was a few girls around. If you couldn't make $1,000 within an hour, there was something seriously wrong. Now the Steel Works have quietened down a lot there's not many guys working in there.

Fran has had a hard life on the street. She was a heroin addict and had lost contact with her children. She told us some

Fran on her chair.

Middle: Governor–General David Hurley answering the door in a re-enactment for the camera.
Bottom: The Gov only does one selfie a day – Anne Louise Rentell, General David John Hurley, AC, DSC, FTSE and me. Australia's Governor–General grew up in Port Kembla. He loved it!

terrifying stories about clients holding her at knife point up alleys and taking her on scary drives. Nevertheless, she still spoke gently about some of her regulars.

Fran: Don't get me wrong. Okay. There are men that can be absolute pigs. But there are true men out there that are, really gentlemans, that are absolutely beautiful.

Another inhabitant of the street, Henri Stephens from 'Spearfishing and Snorkelling – Down Unda' told us in an incredulous tone that a lot of the street workers' clients were 'over fifties'. Perhaps somewhere along the way this tough and functional partnering serves a purpose for both.

There was such a range of characters that appeared as we made the doco, and one person would lead to another. We had to stop somewhere. And that was the Governor–General. Well, to be correct at the time we interviewed him, he was the NSW Governor, soon to be the Australian one. I didn't even know we had a state one before we knocked on the door of NSW Government House in the Domain, a little nervously. He did not answer, but we were ushered into a stately looking room to set up recording gear. We need not have been frightened, he was a true pro.

General David John Hurley, AC, DSC, FTSE: I was born in 1953 and grew up in Port Kembla 'til I was eighteen, there was nothing patriotic about my decision to join the army. My decision to leave Port Kembla was really about not having to work in the steel works if there was an alternative.

These largely unskilled jobs at the steelworks might have put off the young David

Henri Stephens.

Psychic Kerrie Erwin finds a ghost in front of Phillips Tiles in Wentworth Street.

Hurley, but they attracted a huge population of European migrants.

David Hurley: I think growing up in a multicultural society probably prepared me well for later life, because I heard stories about Yugoslavia. I heard stories about Spain. So you had some inkling. We talk about a multicultural Australia, well, that was really multicultural. Sometimes the only language was whistles. You know, when the crane driver whistles or something. Move over here, we got to put this over there. I think one of the beauties of living down that way was you learned about European foods well before it became fashionable in Australia.

As we got deeper into the interview, we realised that the Governor was happy to talk about anything. So knowing that I already had footage of a local psychic, Kerrie Erwin, finding a few ghosts on Wentworth Street, I asked him about whether he believed in the phenomena. He said he didn't 'decry people who believed in such things' and was happy to let the ghosts go beserk in Government House at night, as long as they left him alone. He was also happy to talk about his memories of the Indigenous population in Port Kembla.

David Hurley: When I grew up there, we were aware of them. Because sometimes you'd see humpies in the early days, on the coastal side of the lagoon. And then they had houses built for them. On the southern end of the lagoon. When I grew up in the 'fifties and 'sixties, we had an attitude that was pretty prevalent in those days. We didn't mix with them. A couple of kids came to school. We played sport with them and all that sort of thing, but there was very little social interaction at all. They lived there, and we lived our own life and that was the Australia of the day.

But the Governor was proud of the fact that now, under his charge, Government House flew the Aboriginal flag every day, alongside the Australian flag. To hear the Indigenous side of the story, we met up with Auntie Barbara Nicholson, one of the local Wodi Wodi people, a subgroup of the

Tharawal nation. She is an academic at nearby Wollongong University. We met at her house in Port Kembla, where she gave a warm interview about her life in Port, right back to the depression years.

Henri, from Spearfishing and Snorkelling Down Unda had his thoughts on nearby Coomaditchie Mission, where some Aboriginal people live now.

Henri Stephens: It's very funny. At the end of the day, they've got a settlement. It's got its own rulings, from what I understand they run their own race, it's fine. I have no problem with it. But sometimes I've had the Aboriginals in here, and they say I'm not allowed in the water. What a load of bullshit. But at the end of the day, I think we're carrying on too much with everybody's rights. I think we should be all equal.

Barbara Nicholson: When you look back, you can see how tough life was. But I also look back at the little me and have good memories. It's only really in hindsight, we can see how tough it really was. There was no town water, no sanitary services. We lived in humpies, little shacks built out of whatever material could be gleaned from the local tip. My old Auntie was the last speaker of the language in its pure form. She didn't speak for a long, long time, because up until she died there was no one else to speak it with. One of the sad things with colonisation is that the articles of colonisation made it really hard for Aboriginal people to identify themselves as Aboriginal people. It was actually shameful to do. So, you know, you could be anything. You could be West Indian, you could be Maori, you could be Polynesian, you could be anything. But don't be Aboriginal. If you were Aboriginal you didn't get anything and your kids got taken away.

But there was a real sense of community in Port Kembla. Everyone seemed to know everyone. Lou who ran the Vault Cabaret at the time thought it had an unnecessarily bad name after it fell into decline in the 'eighties.

Lou Belancic: There was a lot of talk about don't go to Port Kembla after dark. Yes there were junkies, but peripheral stuff. There was nothing major, it was just very quiet. You never had a problem getting a car parking space.

Dimi Kapsimallis.

Julie Howard.

So dear drivers, it's not like you have trouble parking there now. You can usually get a park right outside any shop you want to enter. Dimi Kapsimallis from Phillips Tiles, also thought there was a sense of community in the area which she extended to the street workers.

Dimi Kapsimallis: If we see the girls walking around if it's winter. I'll ask how they are or if they're warm enough. And I found that because they knew that we were a stable family here. If ever our back gate had been left unlocked or ajar a little bit they'd say, 'Oh your back doors' a little bit open but don't worry, we make sure that nothing's happened. They keep an eye on businesses after dark.

But of course not everyone in Port likes the street action. We found a café owner, happy to give her side of the story. Perfect for a documentary!

Julie Howard, Enigma Coffee Emporium: It's particularly drugs, it's ice and it's heroin. But that's their lifestyle. By the same token, I don't agree with them impacting on my lifestyle, and how I choose to make my living. So there's no

real interaction. Some of them I'll have a laugh with and talk to. If I get a chance.

By the end of the documentary making process, I felt like I had only just begun to get to know the place. As if you can ever truly know somewhere.

Lou Belancic: Port Kembla people love Port Kembla. And anyone new to the town, basically they feel that. People say 'g'day' in the street, they actually talk to other people about things.

Once we completed the program, together with Claudia Taranto from Radio National, we organised a 'listening event'. Together with some local song and dance performers, we played the program to a group of Port Kembla citizens at the 'servo', a service station that had just been turned into a venue at the time. Most of the audience looked like they were there to see a serious ABC produced documentary about their street. I was a little nervous about their reaction to Henri the spearfishing guy, as he did not know or care what political correctness meant.

Henri Stephens: The weather. It's been like a woman. Lately it's been up and down. You can't really say when you can go for a dive. People say the barrier reef. We have got so much at our doorsteps in this area. It's unbelievable.

This was one of his first 'grabs' and there was a silence that came over the audience. But by the end of it, they were laughing like hyenas at everything he said, even if it wasn't funny.

Henri Stephens: Here. There's a lot of carrots up a lot of people's arses. The people that have the buildings here, they think this streets' going to be worth a million dollars, yes, it might be, but in another twenty years when they're dead!

Okay, time to get back in your car. It won't take long as it's parked right outside Henri's Spearfishing shop in Wentworth Street. It's a steep street, they used to have an annual billy cart derby here. Just follow the road downhill and it will eventually join Highway 1 as it passes near the Nan Tien Temple, one of biggest Buddhist structures in the southern hemisphere. And we're off. Somehow, the giant steelworks and the temple seem to sit well together under the escarpment in this magnificent region.

There's also a classic bit of road you might want to catch on the way out. The sea-cliff bridge. Seen on many car ads. But this shot is from below. Courtesy Amanda Peacock.

SCANDAL RADAR

Why does Port Kembla always have to deal with Sydney's problems? At the start of the COVID-19 pandemic, the *Ruby Princess* was allowed to enter Sydney Harbour by Australian Border Force, even though they were warned there were 440 passengers on board with coronavirus-like symptoms. These passengers disembarked, collected their luggage and dispersed all around Australia! Over 1,400 crew members remained on the ship – 200 were also infected – and the *Ruby Princess* was banished and forced to dock at Port Kembla for ten days. Out of sight, out of mind. An abject failure of government and this incident was the subject of a criminal investigation and special inquiry.

Sections of this chapter can be heard on the *Earshot* documentary, 'Greetings from Port Kembla', ABC Radio National – abc.net.au/rn

OXFORD STREET, SYDNEY

GADIGAL COUNTRY

MUSIC
* *I Feel Love*, Donna Summer
* *What Time is Love*, KLF
* *Step Back in Time*, Kylie Minogue

STAY
Vibe in Rushcutters Bay.

EAT
The Lab Café (great coffee).

POINT OF INTEREST
Oxford Street evolved from an Aboriginal track 'muru' that crossed east along the ridgeline and around the bays to the southern headland of the harbour.

After a pleasant drive down the Princes motorway, we're back in central Sydney in an area that's been thoroughly gentrified. Today it's a twilight zone of a place that's too expensive for its own good. With capital gain, the buildings make as much money empty for the owners as they do with anything going on inside them. We drive past boarded up shops and an odd mix of pedestrians. Wealthy looking dudes look down at their phones as homeless people scream at the traffic.

It was a real life detective story that led me to Oxford Street in Sydney. It's a street I've frequently driven down, walked along and staggered through. The staggering often occurred in the 1980s. The Taxi Club upstairs at the intersection with Bourke Street was a common last drinking stop for many a long night, that might have begun at the Trade Union Club nearby, or many other venues that filled Sydney at the time. There was also the Imperial Hotel over the road that seemed to be open very late. My largely hetrosexual friends would happily carouse the night away, somewhat oblivious to all subcultures nearby. But you could easily end the night dancing with some drag queens. Our interactions with the gay community faded as we got older, but there were shared stories that might lighten up an otherwise dull dinner party. That's how life went, from singing and dancing, and sexual exploration, to children and sitting and drinking and gossiping. That's where I first heard the legend of Trough Man. Whispered, then shouted at gatherings. Not just in my small circle. The story grew 'til it became part of Sydney's unofficial history.

Back, when Oxford Street was having it's hey day from the late 'seventies on, it was sometimes called the 'glittering mile' because of the flashing neon signs and brightly lit gay bars and clubs. There was definitely a wide mix of people using the street – punks, gays, yobbos. The proto-ferals[32] and the homeless were hard to tell apart. My first glimpse of inner city Sydney nightlife was in this area. It seemed both sinister and exciting. At night the street was pumping, Radio Birdman might be playing at Frenches, while Donna Summer was on the turntable at the Saddle Tramp. Disco had travelled from America to Australia, arriving in Oxford Street first. House music followed a couple of decades later with the accompanying metrosexuals. What was a metrosexual? In my mind, these were straight men that dressed like gay ones. They also adopted aspects of their

---

[32] Proto-feral? Have I just made up a category that might have been me in the 1980s.

behaviour. Australian gay culture had come quite a distance over time, from hidden to fashionable. But only in the inner city, and that wasn't all smooth sailing, there was still negativity and violence between the tribes on Oxford Street.

Today metrosexuals are lost in the colourful parade of capital letters that mark our era. The Gay Mardi Gras, which began as a protest march in 1978, became a popular annual event in the 'eighties. There was a period when it was still edgy, but not the mass commercial exercise it became. The metrosexuals and inner city types flocked to it. Oxford Street bars were packed and the Hordern Pavilion at the nearby Sydney showground held the Mardi Gras 'Sleaze Ball'. This became a thumping pleasure dome every year. Ecstasy also came into the mix and as you can imagine, a good time was had by all. There was a wild story that continued to circulate about this era, that many people of a certain age seemed to know.

By the turn of the century, I was living in the Illawarra with my partner Amanda, and two kids. We didn't do that many dinner parties, but on occasion we would indulge. The earlier ones involved a lot more drinking than they would now. Although alcohol remains a core ingredient. I guess it's the closest we can get to those times, when you could drink like a fish, drug like a medical student, and have unrestrained sex like a dolphin.

The Trough Man legend seemed to symbolise those times, even for us hetros. At one particular dinner party, I took the opportunity to interview some guests to get their recollections.[33] Tom and Jill are a couple we met earlier. They are real life friends who have names from a fairy tale, indeed their

33 As you do...

Before and after...

early shots as a couple look like something out of *Blue Lagoon*. This 1980 film is not really a fairy tale, but an adolescent fantasy starring Brooke Shields and a blonde man/boy. Tom and Jill were often participants in the dance scene along Oxford Street in the days before it went super metrosexual.

Tom: It was either a locker room party or the Sleaze Ball. That people would come out of the toilet. Saying, oh my god! Trough Man's there again.

Jill: Everyone would go in, and it would be off putting for a lot of people. And there'd be nowhere else to go. Because you wouldn't go in the cubicles because they would be busy.

But maybe these stories were just told for effect? Perhaps young Tom and Jill's brains were so drug addled they couldn't really remember what was going on. False memories? They didn't seem to have personally seen him, but were convincing in their beliefs. Tom warned me about trying to do a story on him. I was bound to offend someone. I could encounter mental illness. Don't go there! But after this particular dinner party, a couple of the other guests started doing some sleuth work.[34] There was quite a lot about Trough Man on the internet (of course). One of them also had an old boyfriend who had come out as gay during their relationship. He'd claimed to have made a sighting. I called him, and he told me this was true, and described an actual trough encounter, but couldn't remember a name.

By this time, I had convinced Radio National that it would make a good story (somewhat to my surprise). So the following interviews were recorded. Tim Ritchie was a DJ around the scene at the time, who'd ended up at Radio National.

Tim Ritchie, DJ: Whatever his real name was, in the urinal, he was Trough Man, which was a version of Superman. But I think he ended up not surviving. I don't know if the cause was laying in lots of men's urine.

And as I searched for Trough Man, I also found the gay community happy to talk about anything and everything. 'Rat parties' were part of the scene as it grew beyond Oxford Street. Rat parties were originally named after the rodents and then given a more official acronym, Recreational Arts Team as they grew from terrace houses to the Hordern Pavilion. I spoke to Jack Vidgin, who was the main organiser of these events.

Jack Vidgin: Rat parties were a serious gathering of trash. There was nothing like that around before. The Mardi Gras was mainly gay and lesbian people mostly gay, really, because lesbians in those days weren't even that out. The

---

34 Sam and Ivan who you have also heard from earlier.

Rat parties became a bit overlaid with everybody, you know, the average mainstream crowd who would like to go out and party. There was never any trouble between the groups.

Mark Alsop was a gay DJ who worked these big parties.

> **Mark Alsop:** Trough man was something of a legend. I knew that he did exist. It wasn't something made up. However, I never, if I could say, came across him.[35] I'd only ever heard stories about him. And when he was down in the urinals, generally I was working. So my experience with him has not been personal. Although I can urinate on the best of them, so you know, it's not a challenge.

Then I came across an old article in the gay newspaper, *The Star Observer*, about the Sleaze Ball, another huge party held at the Hordern Pavilion every year – post Mardi Gras.

> One thing and one thing alone made my night. It made me forget the awful breeders and my $80 aspro and D.Reams average performance. At Sleaze '94, I had a close encounter with one of the Sydney gay communities legends. I saw Trough Man in action, kneeling in piss and deodorant blocks working his schlong and gleefully waving his free hand in front of other men streams, an urban myth no more.
> Kevin Dixon, *Star Observer*, 1994.

So it seemed like Trough Man did actually exist, at least during the peak of the Sydney warehouse party scene. But there was a lot of mystery around what he actually looked like, maybe as a result of people's drug addled memories and dim toilet lights.

There were tantalising clues on the internet. A video made in the 'nineties. Reported sightings. Could he still be alive? I sent off emails and kept asking awkward questions. Then Gary Wotherspoon, a gay academic, gave me some clear information.

> **Gary Wotherspoon:** Yes, without giving his name away. I know Trough Man, a respected public servant by day, Trough Man by night. And one of my favourite memories of Trough Man, is the early days of the Mardi Gras parties at the Showground, the men's toilet downstairs. They even set up a disco. The lights are off, Trough Man in the trough, and music playing. A moment of atmosphere. There have been Sydney icons of different sorts. I mean Trough Man is certainly representative of a certain lifestyle in Sydney at that time. And many people enjoyed Trough Man's services. There was even a young Trough Man who tried to take over! He didn't last very long. He lacked the panache of Trough Man.

Another Trough Man? People were telling me so many conflicting theories about what did or didn't happen to him. I was confused. I put up a query on a gay Sydney Facebook group. Did anyone have a contact for him?

There was a lot of helpful posts, but nothing that led anywhere. I started editing the story and was about to finish it by letting the listener form their own conclusion. When... an email arrived.

---

35 Spoken with innuendo fully intended.

DRIVE TIME: AUSTRALIAN ROAD GUIDE | GREG APPEL

Dear Greg, I would be happy to contribute. No problem about straight out interview. Barry Charles

And so we met for an interview. We'd had very different lives, starting with very different faces and bodies, but sometimes old men often just end up looking like each other.

Barry Charles: People have been saying I've been dead since about 1998.

Greg Appel: It is quite an honour to meet you.

Barry: Don't do that sort of stuff I'm not comfortable with. Oh, it's entertaining, it's fun to know that people remember it. It brings back all the excitement of that period. For me, the whole period from 1978, from the first Mardi Gras to all the parties that went on, and grew from that. It's a really important part of my life. And it's a very important part of my activism as well. Although people don't understand that I've been involved with the gay rights movement since 1970.

Greg: How did it all begin for you?

Barry: It started when I walked into a New York bar in 1978. And there were hundreds of guys into all sorts of sexual activity and one of them was watersports. And I came back from New York on the tenth of June that year. One of the first things that happened was one of my best friends, who were all gay activists, and politically involved at that stage, said, 'we're having a demonstration on Saturday, but we're making it into a Mardi Gras, we're going to have a party atmosphere to try and generate some activity on Oxford Street and get the non political gays out into the streets.' And I was right up for it. So I put the two things together, discovering my sexual proclivity, which I hadn't been into before then, and my whole political involvement.

Greg: It's an unusual way to become famous. And somehow it seems to be quite a Sydney thing. You're like the wild extreme of things that went on at these parties and people are thinking back to happier times for themselves. Do you think that's right?

Barry: I think it is. I think as we moved into the late 'nineties, I used to say that the parties became sanitised. When Fox Studios took over the Showground, there were all sorts of rules about public liability insurance and all these sorts of issues. You just weren't allowed to do that sort of thing anymore. So I was part of this wild era, where there weren't all these kinds of restrictions. And I can remember the last Mardi Gras party I went to, and the security just came in and shut the whole thing down. There was a whole group of us playing around. And by then I had a few acolytes who were doing the same thing as me. And we just got kicked out, you know, basically, it just wasn't the party anymore. So I stopped going.

Greg: So you became an OH&S issue?

Barry: Yes, I think so. Because of the crowds. I mean, basically, because of the number of people that used to accumulate around the scene...

Greg: All right, well, let's go through some of the rumours I've heard about, like you were dead.

Barry: In the mid to late 'eighties and early 'nineties. People were dying in large numbers. So people who were not engaged with the scene kind of identified anyone who was doing something out of the ordinary must get the disease. And so rumours started to circulate that I must have died as a result. Because I wasn't quite as visible in the late 'nineties as I had been. By then I was in my late forties. And I just couldn't do it all the time. And a couple of people, much younger men took over from me at that stage. The rumour just spread that I was dead.

Greg: That's the other rumour – that there was another Trough Man.

Barry: There certainly was, initially a guy from Brisbane. And then my favourite one is the guy from Wellington in New Zealand, who's a good deal younger than me and he was a worthy successor. Let me tell you.

Greg: Some people are describing your outfit almost like you're a superhero. Can you remember what you wore?

Barry: I had sort of army fatigues. And I got that from a guy at the club in 1978, who had a pair of olive green army fatigues and that's all he wore. And he said, I never wash these. He said I just put them in the dryer. And I decided to try and emulate that.

Trough Man looked alive and well to me. Maybe he was a superhero. People looking for the next wellness fad need look no further.

Barry: I've had some doctor's advice over the years and they basically say that urine is pretty clean. It has so many other minerals and chemicals in it that it nullifies a lot of things. Even though it's waste, it's pretty pure, and I've never had a problem with it over all those years. I've never had anything.

You can hear all this evidence and more via ABC Radio National. The story made quite a splash! You can hear it online at 'In search of Trough Man, an icon of Sydney's 1980s gay scene'. My main worry was whether the gay community would accept me making the story and that Trough Man himself would not be so happy with my general tone.

But I had nothing to worry about, from the comments I received, the community seemed to really enjoy it. Like me, they thought it was an important part of Sydney's history. I was actually relieved to get some good old hetro troll abuse. Sadly, a sure sign that a story is cutting through.

HIGHWAY 1 REVISITED

As much as we look to the outback to define us, Australia is a nation of people who enjoy living squashed together, preferably by the coast, preferably in the more temperate regions. The true Australian probably lives five floors up in an anonymous apartment built in the last twenty years. Or perhaps it's in an anonymous suburb? On our all seeing road trip, how do we deal with these cities? There are long car journeys between all of them, but even though we are finding meaning in our boredom, I think we would go beyond a critical pain threshold if I described every one of those journeys in any sort of detail. Lets just try an impressionistic version.

Big Things: An Ode to Highway 1

Big Banana	Big Dog on a Tuckerbox
Big Lobster	Big Axe
Big Potato	Big Bull
2 x Big Pineapples	Big Koala
3 x Big Oranges	Big Kookaburra
Big Peach	Big Tassie Devil
Big Apple	Big Pelican
Big Cherries	Big Penguin
Big Mandarin	Big Bottle
Big Fruit Bowl	Big Wine Cask
Big Macadamia	Big Cheese
Big Peanut	Big Lollipop
Big Merino	Big Easel
Big Ram	Big Milkshake
Big Wool Bales	Big Miner
Big Golden Guitar	Big Rocking Horse
Big Guitar	Big Root
Big Galah	Big Earthworm
Big Cassowary	Big DNA
Big Barramundi	Big Arch of Victory
Big Trout	Big Captain Cook
Big Murray Cod	Big Gold Panner
Big Crab	Big Ned Kelly
Big Prawn	Big Gumboot
Big Shell	Big Stubbie
Big Croc	
Big Chook	

MUSIC
* *My Island Home*, Warumpi Band, the original and to me, the best version.
* *Nutbush City Limits*, Tina Turner (and check out the Drive Time podcast first Christmas special on this subject).
* *Tessellate*, alt-J (I was stuck in a car on a long trip with one CD a few years back. It's the only way that anything new gets to me. thank goodness it was this one).

STAY
The Parkroyal, Darling Harbour. If you get a view across the freeways to Darling Harbour, you'll really feel a part of the freeway experience. And you can see Highway 1 in all it's spidery glory as it twists up into itself to cross Sydney Harbour.

EAT
At Humble Pie, 1 Mogo Place, Billinudgel.

VISIT
Sydney Opera House, might as well get along the biggest big thing in Australia, it's where they hold the Australian Slam Poetry Championship every year.

RANDOM POINT OF INTEREST
Australia has the most big things per capita than anywhere else in the world. A fact based on speculation and light arithmetics.

Australian slam champion 2014, Zohab Zhe Khan, food tips for the road: "nuts, tuna, spinach are my holy trinity".

How's that for an Australian beat poem! In random categorical order. Which brings me to the big thing that I saw all burned down. It was that fateful year of 2018. As part of my eclectic line of work, I was on tour filming champion Slam Poets for on online series.[36] Slam poets are kind of modern beat poets, who get up and perform their short poems to an audience that sometimes clicks their fingers. Zohab Zee Khan is the kind of performer that gets them clicking. He grew up on the Riverina and can work any crowd, anywhere.

Zohab: I don't think there's that many people that get to travel around and make a living speaking poems out of their mouth. So I'm definitely one of the lucky ones because I'm on the road like 300 plus days of the year.

It was on the road with Zohab that I picked up our food tips for this chapter. Well it was actually via Zohab and a very 'relaxed' Christine Anu.[37] We bumped into her in a bar, on the road, Zohab's true home.

Zohab: I was hanging out with Christine Anu and she gave me the best piece of advice when it comes to roadside food. She said there's a little town just north of Byron Bay called Billinudgel. And it's the home of the humble pie. So probably you should go check out the humble pie place.

There's a huge network of places around Australia and the world where slam poets ply their trade. They also run competitions where the same finger clicking audience votes. Australia has an organisation called Word Travels that I happened to have made

36 This calls for a link to illustrate: youtu.be/RKhWRHMwaik

37 She covered 'My Island Home' at Olympic Games in Sydney and all that.

videos for, over quite a few years. They hold the Australian Slam poetry championship at the Sydney Opera House every year. I have therefore become familiar with the genre. To the point where I know it's possible my own slam poem 'Big Things' a couple of pages back, might win 7.2 points out of ten, or even more on a good night. Depends on my delivery of course and whether the audience sees the work for its ironic value rather than offensive. Age is no barrier, there's plenty of old people having a go amongst the younger generation. It's all part of the art form. In fact, the bushy bearded types delivering an old fashioned bush poems are very popular.

But on the road in NSW, along Highway 1 just north of Newcastle, myself and some real slam poets, came across the recently incinerated Big Rock. It was built by Australia's TV tourist pioneers the Leyland Brothers in 1990 when Uluru was called Ayers Rock.

There is also a bit of a backstory to this burnt fibreglass shell. The year before, I had been on the same annual slam poetry mission. After winning, the Australian national slam champion would tour the regional areas, spreading the slam word. I would be there to capture the action on HD video. On this trip we visited the shopping centre inside this same replica rock. After filling up with petrol under the handy artificial rock overhang, one of the poets, a visiting American Australian Slam Poetry champion,[38] Arielle Cottingham found a shop selling golliwogs inside this big thing. It seemed archaic and offensive. The sort of material that often finds its way into slam poetry. Perfect material for us to film a little seg-

ARIELLE COTTINGHAM
APS CHAMPION, 2016
POET, PERFORMANCE ARTIST

ment for the slam poets on tour series. The store owner saw us with the camera and sensed negative press. She chased us out of the mall. So when I returned with the next years slam poetry champion, Jesse Oliver, we filmed the smoldering ruin for a sequel. Somehow an appropriate end to the Big Rock and what it represented and perhaps

---

38 Confusing, but it's possible to be a foreign born national and win the Australian Slam Poetry championship as Arielle Cottingham did in 2016.

DRIVE TIME: AUSTRALIAN ROAD GUIDE | GREG APPEL

Adult Australian Slam Poetry Champion 2017 Jesse Oliver checks out the Big Banana.

it should be a line at the end of my own Big Things slam poem. 'Big Burnt Rock' Not to belittle the joy that these big things can generate. The good old big banana still remains innocently innuendoey.[39]

The journey to find Australia's Slam Champion continues every year. The competition attracts outsiders, seekers, frustrated comedians, exhibitionists, the old, the young and people from all over the world. In 2021, during a kind of break in the Coronavirus pandemic that didn't quite cover all states, there was a mixture of large stage and zoom performances that made up the interstate finals. The winner turned out to be a young Sudanese refugee holed up in her Brisbane bedroom. Huda 'the Goddess' had fled to Australia after a difficult life in Sudan.

The winning announcement sent her and her friends into absolute raptures on the bed. It was a moment where live online broadcast and old school cameras on tripods (me), came together symbiotically. Not always the case with the layers of technology we all struggle under.

To do justice to the large cities of Australia, again, we can only make an impressionistic attempt.

39 A new word meaning the potential for innuendo is huge!

Scraggly Old Geezer Poem: The Capital Cities 2021

Sydney sin city is full of the virus
Gladys not happy but we've still got the Opera house
Melbourne the rival may now be victorious
Dan is the man goes the Victorian hypothesis
He could bring us together again
If we would just do the right thing
Or is our new leader from another state
They've kept out the virus by shutting the gates
Who'd ever heard of these people before
Xenophobia wins votes
Shut that vacuum sealed door
Perth McGowan Brisbane Palaszczuk
Adelaide Marshall Darwin Gunner
Hobart Gutwein
Even Canberra has one,
Andrew Barr
But does the rest of the country know him?
That might be going a bit too far.[40]

Australia is a suburban country and many of us live in the endless non-descript suburbs that ring the capitals. Yet these places aren't nondescript to people who live in them. In fact if you look closely they can be quite different. The suburb I grew up in is as good an example as any. Garran, in the Woden Valley, in Canberra. To me, it was full of meaning, every rock, tree, bus stop, shop and storm water drain. Yet to people from elsewhere it's part of the vast bland fields of houses that sprawl across this city. The suburb next door to us called

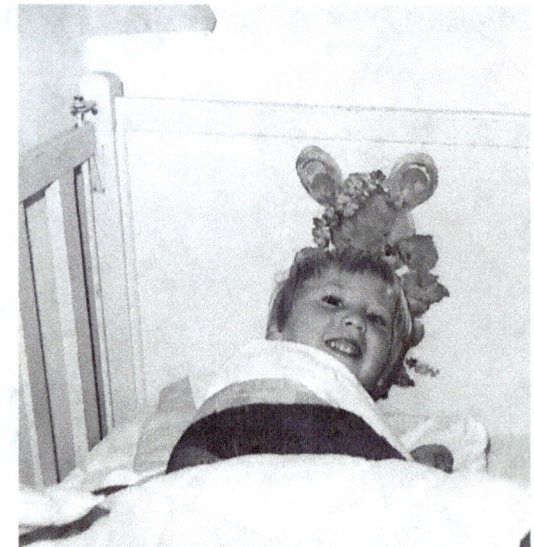

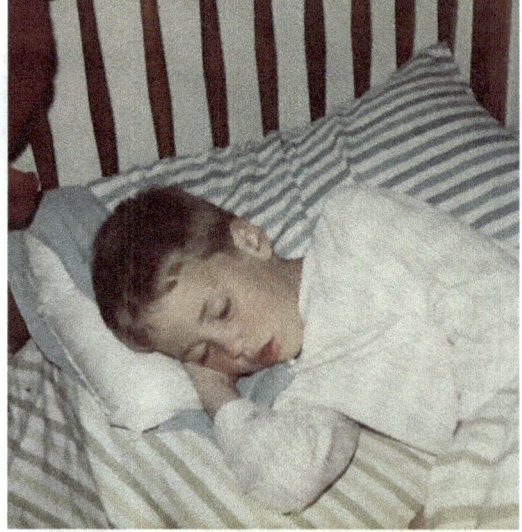

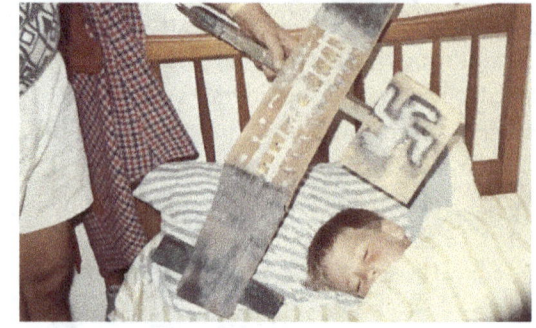

Inside the suburban dream in Garran, Canberra, ACT

40 This dated the second I wrote it.

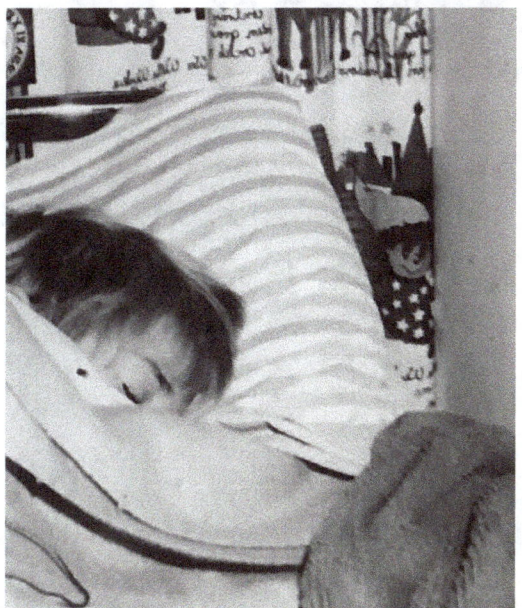

SCANDAL RADAR

Australia prides itself on the 'big' things – perhaps to remind us that this really is a big country: it's the sixth largest country in the world by land mass (that's the loud part) but only the fifty-fifth by population (that's the quiet part). And nobody is going to take anything big away from us. The Ballina Shire Council decided to remove one of these icons – the Big Prawn – in 2009, and faced an uproar, including protests and representations to the Council – and 6,000 signatures on a Facebook petition. Australia has destroyed much flora and fauna since white settlers arrived in 1788 but the community decided enough is enough and swung into action to save this prawn made from concrete and fibreglass. Classic Australian-style environmental activism. The Council never acted upon its original decision and the Big Prawn wasn't demolished – but faced an uncertain future until Bunnings purchased the Big Prawn for $21 million in 2014! Oh, and the adjoining land which enabled Bunnings to build yet another Bunnings Warehouse. But at least it meant the survival of one massive prawn.

Hughes, was a completely different world to me as a child. Today, I drive through and realise they're exactly the same. Canberra does a good job of representing a suburban nation by architectural example.

THE SUBURBS

CAR YARDS ON THE EDGE OF TOWN

THE SUBURBS

MUSIC
* *Running Up That Hill*, Kate Bush. Sounds like the edges of suburbia, where the city meets the countryside.
* *I Hate the Music*, John Paul Young. One of his classics all about a suburban romance.
* *Gargoyle*, the Lighthouse Keepers.

STAY
Ibis Budget Casula Liverpool, 437 Hume Highway.

EAT
McDonald's. I must say out of all these kind of places, McDonald's hangs in there. You know what you're getting. I remember the excitement in Canberra when the first one came. A bit like the internet. Little did we know.

VISIT
HomeWorld Box Hill, these places are pretty amazing and if you visit them like a museum of nowadays, you're in for a treat

RANDOM POINT OF INTEREST
In the book *The Lucky Country*, Donald Horne claims Australia as the first suburban country.

John Paul Young doing a bit of press for *Van Park*, 2012.

I might have grown up in the suburban capital, but my experience of Australia's hard core suburbs was limited. I moved to Sydney in the 'eighties and was often driving up the Hume. To get to the middle where all the inner city types lived you had to go through the outskirts. Liverpool and places such as these. They looked much more scary than Canberra.

But we're going to detour into this area right now. Who better to take us there than John Paul Young. A Glaswegian sheet metal worker who became known around Australia as 'JPY'. If a name is not short enough to add an 'o' to, Australians love to initialise. JPY is a man who loves cars, and when I first started working with him on my musical *Van Park*, he'd been enjoying them so much that he'd lost his licence for a while.

We've already met him earlier, when he got off the boat in Perth on his way to Sydney. Compared to Glasgow, John found Sydney innocent. And he was just eleven years old.

JPY: Sydney was just a big country town. We arrived on Australia Day in 1962 and you could have fired a gun down George Street and you would not have hit one person. You wouldn't have seen one flag to save your life. It was just Australia Day, beach day.

As so often happens in this story, people are firing guns down the main street. Strangely, the flags have come and then started to go again. Australia Day is now very confused and on the brink of collapse. It's all part of the story isn't it co-drivers? John and his family were taken out to the western suburbs of Sydney to begin their new life.

JPY: In Glasgow when I was eleven years old, I had a three-piece Italian suit with cloth buttons and pointy toe shoes. In Australia, I was sitting on the banks of the Williams Creek in a pair of shorts wondering what the hell had happened to me. I mean, I was enjoying it. I was dragged back from the brink of becoming an adult at twelve and I found my childhood again which was just bloody marvellous. I felt like a real city kid. In Glasgow, I had girlfriends and everything. It was just bizarre at ten years old. We would go to the dams on a Saturday afternoon. You grew up very quickly in the UK.

The Youngs were taken to the East Hills Migrant Centre. Then the family got shifted to housing in the nearby suburb of Liverpool. It was full of other migrants.

JPY: I can't remember why, but there was a whole shift of people from the inner city suburbs like Petersham, who moved out to the western suburbs as well. But we didn't meet that many of these Aussies. There were a few, but compared to the Italians and the Scots and the English, no. Not many at all.

When John finally went to inner city Sydney to work at Alberts Studios and begin his career as a pop star, it was a whole different world. The furniture was different.

JPY: Ohh, extensive leather and wood. I knew I had stepped over a line. I'd crossed a boundary into a different world because I was still a sheet metal worker out in the western suburbs. It was very different for me because I lived all my life in the suburbs and we rarely got into town. If we did, it was night time.

In the 1970s, the artist/musician Blak Douglas grew up in Blacktown in the western suburbs of Sydney, as it was beginning to sprawl. Safely tucked away in middle class Canberra, this area was a 'no go' zone. I asked Blak if it really was as scary as I imagined when we drove past as children.

Blak Douglas: Of course, it was terrifying. I lived in the nightmare of Australiana. Which was homophobic, misogynistic, bonehead culture. If you didn't wear black Levi's, desert boots, and a flannelette shirt with the sleeves cut off, then you were in danger walking down the main street of Penrith. Particularly Thursday nights whenever they'd go to the shops. And what kind of deadshit society is that? But I was kind of fortunate, because I was connected to the guys that weren't afraid to retaliate. There was quite a population of Aboriginal mob in the area when I was growing up. And it was always the same. They were trouble and stay away from them. It was all right for me because I don't physically look like the other mob that was at school. The dark mob copped constant shit from the bogan white kids. Every day was a battlefield.

Even in Canberra we had heard about these bogans, ours were called booners (or hoons). In Sydney, this suburban breed were called 'Westies'. Blak is related to the famous Aboriginal boxers from Kempsey, the Sands brothers. He knew how to throw a punch and so did his dad.

Blak Douglas: I was proud because my dad was Aboriginal. He was a pretty mean mofo. He looked like JJ the father on *Good Times* when he was angry. And you don't want to mess with a black fella like that. So all my mates were scared of him. He was this menacing force, and he'd been a pub brawler all his life. What happens is you're at a pub, you're trying to enjoy a quiet drink, your wife's the barmaid and a bunch of dickhead drunkards cotton on to what's going on. And then they've had one too many towards the end of the night. Everyone wants to fight the black guy. And that still exists in many country towns.

The western suburbs fashion sense doesn't sound that different from the Woden Plaza, which was our local shopping mall in Canberra. Ugg boots, flannelette jackets were the look. There was a certain homogeneity to Australian culture in this period, with differing degrees of viciousness. Car culture made suburbia a little more bearable. You could escape somewhere or at least inside the vehicle.

Blak Douglas: Being a bonafide 'Westie', cars are in the blood. One must remember that when I was 'knee high to a grasshopper', cars were unconsciously COOL! Even if undesirable, they still had character unlike today's average civilian vehicle. My first car was a Morris Mini Deluxe and back in the 'eighties, they were a dime-a-dozen. As I write this, there's a stable of five vehicles which I consider my 'nest eggs'. As I don't have superannuation, I kid myself that these particular vehicles shall contribute to my well-being later in life.

I think my fantasy version of the western suburbs can be glimpsed in this story I wrote in the late 'eighties. It's about that inner city–suburban divide. Of course, it's fiction and some of it does not ring true. It also reads like a short story that would be howled down in a writing class these days. At the time, it certainly wasn't. For a start, my only real experience of these suburbs was being in bands that attempted to play there. Anywhere outside of our sheltered inner city enclave of forgiving venues was hard going. Hang in there dear drivers.

This story does have cars.

SCANDAL RADAR

The ugg boot might be a fashion choice of the mighty western suburbs of Sydney and a classic Australian icon, but suffered from identity theft during a trademark battle between a massive US company, Deckers Outdoor, and a littl' ol' Australian business, Australian Leather. In a five-year legal case, a US Appeals Court decided "UGG Australia" is, indeed, an American brandname owned by Deckers Outdoors – registered in the US in the 1980s – which means that no Australian-made ugg boot can ever enter the shores of America and be sold.

 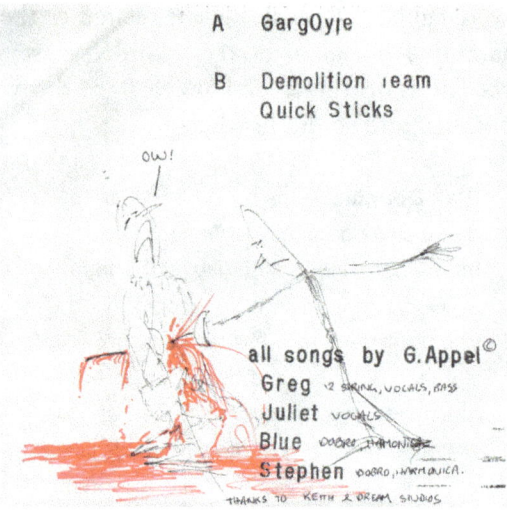

Swordfighting seemed to be a common theme in my creative work. From a hand-drawn Lighthouse Keepers single cover I did back in the day. Although the song is unconnected it seems to work with this story.

SWORDFIGHTING

by G Appel (1988-ish)

My trouble was that I had things inside me that I couldn't get out. I began to think that this was everyone's problem round these parts. We just walked around with a mean look on our faces, not saying much.

These parts. These parts weren't anywhere. I wasn't even that sure of the name of where I lived. If you wanted to write me a letter, which you wouldn't, I couldn't tell you where to send it. It was just somewhere out of town. Country people didn't like us, and city people didn't like us any better. Well they can get fucked.

We didn't like each other that much either.

It had been a good year for a change. There was a bit of work around, and a bit more money. Enough, so you weren't thinking about it all the time; and not thinking about money all the time, got me to thinking about other things. Like I wasn't getting any younger, and I wanted to get out, and it was time to find a woman. Why? Because I hadn't had a fuck for on a year, and my dick was beginning to hurt. The girls round here didn't like me. Well they can get fucked.

And not thinking about money, made me think about the things I couldn't get out.

Friday night. I get in the Ute: new set of mags, half finished paint-job; I head into town.

I hadn't been there since I lived with the old man, and then we didn't go much, except to the zoo or some cunt of a thing. Anyway, I was sick of hanging round with blokes at the petrol station taking in traffic fumes and talking about fuck all; because basically they were all cunts.

It took a long time to get in. It was further

than I remembered. I kept thinking, what do all these cunts in these fucking buildings, do? Isn't there enough stuff around already? And thinking about all of them in these flats and houses, was enough to cause pain. Maybe the world is suffering from overpopulation or the likes.

Anyway, I waited till I was right in the middle, big buildings all around. Because I had this idea that I wanted to be in the centre, because that was where everything of importance happened; and I thought maybe if I could find a woman here and fool her into thinking I was from a fancy area, she might let me root her. Then this line of thinking got me worried about my manner of dress, which might set me apart from some of the other blokes I could see walking around, and make me less desirable as a result.

And hadn't it changed, since me and the old man went to the zoo. Well if you take that line of thought, maybe they'd opened a few of the enclosures and made it like a drive-in situation.

There was a lot of weird looking cunts in these central parts; but then there were a few I wouldn't stick my dick into back home. The whole fucking lot of them.

I saw a place with a few spunks going into it, and decided this must be the centre of the universe. So I held my breath and went in. Fuck me if they didn't start staring at me straight off. At least I thought they were. I could feel their eyes on me, but I couldn't catch them. Otherwise I would have confronted them with the situation. But I suppose back home it would have turned a few heads, if any of these freaks had turned up at the pub. In fact, come to think of it, we would have been a whole lot more uncivilised about it; but then this was a civilised area. Fuck off, these cunts didn't look like they'd be designing any pyramids tonight. In fact they didn't look like they could see one, and I wondered how so much standing up was going on.

I thought to myself, if I wanted to get lucky I'd better put some spade work in, straight away before I threw up or something. So I put in an all out performance; you know, trying to light girls smokes and grabbing their arses and stuff. But they were definitely not biting. Before I got overcome with depression, I retreated into the corner with a couple of double rum and cokes, and decided to observe and reassess.

And what went on before my eyes, began to give me a sick feeling after a while, that all was not right with these people. The blokes weren't even trying to come onto the womenfolk; who were either too out of it, or talking at a frightening speed at some poor bastard; who was either too out of it to answer back, or looking around the room at other cunts looking about. Maybe they didn't want to wear their glasses on account of looking like a fuckwit, or something. Now I know there's a lot of homosexuality and the like going on in these parts, but I'm sure not all of these cunts were lesos and poofters; basically, like everyone else stalking the face of the planet, they were out to get a root. But they went about it in a very strange manner.

Then I saw her. Lying on the floor, looking very peaceful compared to a few minutes back; and looking rather attractive to a man in my state of mind and marital status. No one seemed to miss the last section of the high pitched tirade, that she was delivering in a previously upright position. I thought to myself; am I that much of a low, depraved bastard. And the answer came back: too fucking right I am.

And as she began to re-enter the land of the living; and my bristly face, taking up a large percentage of her field of vision, came into focus; I could see all sorts of paranoid thoughts moving about in her head. She let out a little squawk. I mean, this was where they got all the best headlines from, I suppose. It was rather a bright sort of a day, and things out here look kind of sharp and nasty in a particular sort of light.

"Coffee." I asked, to break the silence.

"A... yes, thank you." she says, nervously reaching for the first cigarette.

"Here." I already had a fairly warm one ready.

"Oh... thank you." not looking like she was going to drink much of it... if you don't mind me asking, where am I?"

"You've passed into the after-world," I said with what I thought was a friendly smile."and after doing the figures, I decided you were due for a spell in Liverpool." this wasn't going down well. "Don't worry I'm not going to hurt you or anything."

She looks at me with absolute terror. "What's the time?" "Don't know."

"Look, I don't know what's happened and I appreciate everything you've done, but I think I'd better be going. I'm meant to be somewhere today and this friend, we're meant to be looking for a house, she'll kill me, I let her down last week..."

"Eh, calm down. Honest, I wouldn't hurt you. I can get you back all right. You don't have to make excuses. I know what I look like to you, but I'm a pacifist, you know? Peace and love are as basic to me as a dick and two testicles full of willing semen. I just thought, you know, after we'd been intimate, you could be a little more polite."

This seemed to fill her with a fresh dosage of horror. She started running her fingers wildly through her hair and hyperventilating on the cigarette.

"We didn't...? Look I'm sorry if there's been a misunderstanding, I was pretty out of it, last night. You don't always know what you're doing, I just don't remember anything..."

"I'm having you on. Look I saw you there, astral travelling on the floor; and I admit some of my thoughts were less than pure, and yes I wanted a root that bad I was vibrating, and I asked you if you wanted a lift out of that hole, and I got no reply. What was I meant to do?"

"You could have left me there. Didn't anyone try and stop you?"

"Not a one. I don't think they could see that far. You don't know what might happen in this day and age. I couldn't just leave you there, could I?

"You certainly could have."

"I was in love."

"I'm scared, can't you see? You had no right..."

"I'm sorry, what can I say. I had a bit of a hard on, but I got the white stuff out in the bog and everything. I didn't even have a look, although it went against what the lizard told me."

This seemed to stun her into complete silence, and desperately I tried to make amends.

"It's sort of nice having you in here. It makes it a bit different, you know. Maybe it's something to do with your tits, a few circular things in the house."

Here she let out a short scream, culminating in a sort of a no, noise at the end.

"I'm sorry, I'm sorry. We don't seem to

understand each other, we've got a bit of an accent round here. What have I done?"

"Look don't worry, maybe I'm overreacting, maybe I'm not overreacting."

"Perhaps I'm using too many short words for you." "No no, don't get all defensive."

"Give me ten minutes, that's all. I promise nothing'll happen to you."

"I would consider it honestly. I mean thanks for everything, I don't know why I have to get to the point of unconsciousness every night. But I'm not making excuses, I've been putting this guy off for a week."

"It was female a minute back."

"No no, this is different, that was for the house. I'm meant to be meeting these guys at Ferricio's, in town."

"A whole pack of the beggars now. I'm sorry, you are busy."

"All right I'm a bit vague this morning. My brain's a bit addled."

"Look I'll put all the sharp things in the shed. Let me make you a proper fry up. I don't often get to meet anyone like you. I mean, put it down to a scientific experience."

"Think yourself lucky."

"What's that meant to mean?"

"It means you'd be much better off, not meeting anyone like me."

"I think what you mean is, you'd be better off."

"No it isn't actually."

"Why would anyone want to have anything to do with a no-hoper like me's, more the question? You think I'm from another planet, right?"

"No, of course not."

"Get fucked you lying bitch."

"If you want me to stay another second, you'll have to tone down some of the sexist terminology."

"All right, just get fucked then." And finally she smiled.

"I'm sorry, it just goes against everything I believe in. It hurts to hear those words together in the same sentence."

"Fine, so it doesn't look like you want your coffee. Let's try you out on beer. Ease you into the day. Right?"

A look of consideration was enough.

We got on all right. Actually we got on fine. I think I was more surprised than she was. But after a little digging, and a little pushing, we discovered we weren't that different. It's a bit hard for me to talk about the good things, seeing as a bad word always seems to come into my mouth before a good one. But sometimes I think these words are only bad, because people get so pissed off when they're not getting enough of them. Like most of the people, all the time.

I just remember strange little pictures, of what I will have to admit was a romance.

A waterfall. I can smell her. I can see her face changing slightly every day. I can feel her skin, so soft after being alone with my own ape-like extremities, for so long. And so pale, like it had never been in the sun. And the shapes printed on it of a morning, creases and contours.

And all the time, she just kept talking to me. Even though I didn't say much. Slowly, I began to tell her a few things I never told anybody. But she just kept talking, and once we'd exhausted your basic subject matter, we went into a freeform manner of speech; and would talk about anything that descended from the sky.

We only had one disagreement, if you could call it that, in that first month we were together; and we were together night and day.

I had a couple of swords, I don't know why, I suppose they were an attempt at decoration or something. She made some comment about phalluses or whatever and got one down. She began pretending to come at me with it. So I got the other one, and we started mucking around. We were doing it like in a movie, and doing a fine job of it too, rolling about, heaving backwards and forwards, grunting and groaning. And all of a sudden someone got hurt, and it became serious. We started to try and hurt one another. I started to become angry. She started kicking me. Then I got overtaken with this wild desire to actually stick it into her, and I could see she was thinking the same. Almost like if we killed the other one now, they would go out happy. Like this was the moment, before everything turned bad. Then my own strength got me and I bashed her sword away. She was looking at me scared, but wanting me to hit her as well. Then I handed my sword to her; we looked at each other for a moment. Then I leaped on her and we fell on the ground laughing and touching and stuff. It was only a moment, but it was a long one. Maybe we missed it.

One night we're sitting inside, by the heater as usual. We've had a bit of a powerful number, and I drift off into the solar system. As I look down from space I can see the lights, things look all right for a change; the traffic and the factories have stopped for the night. People are in their houses watching tele or sleeping or whatever. I can hear her voice rising up to me, because I know it so well; like a mother hears a baby. When she's a bit out of it, she starts to change her accent; you know, a posh voice, or someone out of the movies. But I don't mind, everyone is allowed a few disgusting habits, and I know what her real voice is anyway. Slowly I descend to be with it, seeing as she gets narked when I don't listen to what she's saying.

"The trouble with men is that they don't like women. They try because they need them. They try and try, but they're alone in the end. I thought maybe they had some sort of secret sect for a while; but they don't, they don't have anyone. They're competing against each other. If only they could stop and see they're of the same species, and everyone isn't out to get them. Maybe they are, maybe they're right. Maybe I just hate them. I try and I try. But there's no hope; from the skinniest, palest, wettest ones to the biggest, ugliest ones. I want them to love me, but they won't be in it. They love my body, they don't love me, and I don't want what they have to offer, because it's nothing. And when I get old and dry up, it equals nothing. I've had them to the point where they nearly break, then they just close up and turn back into the minerals they're made of. And if it wasn't for me they'd have nothing, they'd get nothing. They can have their own bums, because I've had enough of nothing. I'm hurt and I can't do it anymore."

I put in the odd appropriate grunts to show I'm listening. But my eyes are rolling around in my head a little, on account of the noxious substances reeking havoc throughout my central nervous system.

"I was out with him one night, or I thought I was meant to be. I said, "I've had enough of this. Do you love me?" He said, "Of course, of course." I said, "Then why are you fucking her and her, and that one over there?" He says, "I didn't." I say, "Stop right there, you're lying out and out." And on and on it goes. And they go on about their space, and I go on about my space, and it all equals nothing, etc etc. Take some more of this darling, and then I fucking hate you more the next day, so fuck off. Excuse me, sorry I'm getting a bit hysterical. Calm down. But sometimes I think perhaps we should call the experiment off, because I don't want to be part of it, and I don't know anyone who's happy with it. No, maybe a few, but they're one celled creatures; maybe that's the way to be. No, maybe there's a few others, but the percentages are horribly low. When you take into account; all the starving hoards, the oppressed (here she puts up her fingers and makes the punctuation, then makes an argh noise and looks at her fingers in disgust), the sick, the deformed, then to top it off; the miserable: poor and miserable, scraping by and miserable, rich and miserable and just plain miserable. We must be looking at a figure with a decimal point by now. And how do you get into that lucky fraction? Buddhism? Windsurfing? Don't ask me."

"No, hang-gliding," I says.
"Gardening," she says
"Big game fishing."
"Oceanography."
"An enormous cock."
"A consuming interest in quantum mechanics."
"A bottomless steak."
"Icecream."
"A pig."
"What do you mean a pig?"
"Just a pig."
"No a dog with a stable home life."
"No a cat...with..."
"Yes I know, a big cock. How about a planet, a nice blue one with twenty moons, in a nice warm part of the galaxy... two suns..."
"Yes, I think I've been there..."

I don't know why. Suddenly it all became too much for me. I suppose I'd been on my own for too long. I'd become set in my ways, or whatever the old excuse is. Her presence began to irritate me. I got sick of being told what was wrong with me. At first I didn't mind being challenged about everything, it made life a bit interesting as opposed to sitting by yourself thinking mean things. But it became a bit much, being told everything I thought and said was wrong. I mean everything couldn't be wrong. Why was she so right about everything. Her voice went from a reasonably interesting drone, to a high pitched chainsaw. Her face seemed to get uglier, and I saw a nagging old woman in there. I knew it wasn't the kind of thing you could tell someone politely, and it would bring on a severe outburst of earbashing; perhaps with more reason this time. No, I didn't want to talk about it. I decided on a different course of action.

I knew the only way to get rid of her was to introduce a psychic aspect into the household. I began to conjure up the demons that I knew all city folk thought inhabited these parts.

I took to eating raw meat with no veg, and smearing the blood on my face in the style of Java man. I tipped bottles of scotch down the sink and over my head, and left them lying around for her to find. I took to pulling strange expressions, making little noises and staring at her blankly. I let myself become dirty and bearded. I spent a lot of time on the roof, occasionally poking my head from above, into the living room window. But I never laid a hand on her, or stepped over the limits of what was acceptable behaviour to a woman of her stature. She didn't think to ask me what I was doing. She must have just thought she didn't know me as well as she thought.

After a while this began to take the bark out of her. It was almost pleasant for a while. She began to complain less and took on a pale downcast look, if you could imagine her any paler. I began to feel sorry for her. I wondered why she didn't just leave.

One day I caught her crying in the kitchen, and it broke my heart. I realised I was caught up in her in a way I hadn't realised. It was an entirely new emotion for me, and it scared me. Maybe I was just scared of her.

"What's up?"

"I just don't know what's happening."

"It's my fault; I suppose I'm trying to hurt you."

"Why. What have I done wrong? Just tell me that."

"Nothing..."

"Do you want me to go... I thought it was good... I thought you liked me..."

"It's not that. Maybe it is. It's just sort of, all new to me, it's all a bit much. You don't know how long I've been on my own, you know. You get used to it. Now it's like I can't cope. I don't know how to explain...it's just like all this talking. What does it mean? It gets on my nerves...I'm not used to it."

"But I thought you wanted someone to talk to. I thought I was giving you something you needed."

"I don't know."

"You don't realise we're the same. I'm just the same; but I can say to you, "I need you". But you can't, can you? It's just such a waste. We were that close, all you had to do was make the smallest of efforts. Of course you get tired of me, who wouldn't? It's normal, why can't you be brave enough to open up a little. Make yourself vulnerable. Just say it to me... you can't, can you? You're just going to let me go, aren't you? You bastard, you're going to sit there aren't you? Well I tried. I tried for you and I tried for me and I'm giving in. Goodbye...I don't believe this... goodbye..."

And she walked away.

I sat there wallowing in my own thoughts. Darkness descended and the earth pulled down hard on me. I kept thinking about all the good things we had, as compared to the horrible loneliness that held me now. I sat there for a good half an hour. It was like something was missing from my body. I'd never felt anything like it before. I was really scared now.

Then suddenly I get up and bolt. Running like a mad cunt through the streets. Past all the houses and factories and shops. Till I get to the highway. Then I see her over the other side of the road. I yell out at her at the top of my voice.

"Stop! Come back. Please!"

She turns around and sees me. I run across the road. A truck gets me. Then a car. Then another. Then a bus.

* * *

And so we get some random vehicles appearing. I've seen that ending used in a TV series or two. But I had not seen it when the story was written in the late 'eighties. I find that story difficult to read now, I think I always did, but it has its twists and turns, not all of them bad. But let's not go backwards. Onward we drive. Let's have a quick look at some very different communities and their histories in different Australian towns.

BATHURST
WIRADJURI COUNTRY

MUSIC
* *Emu Strut,* the Flying Emus
* *Highway Star,* Deep Purple
* *Isa Brown,* Genni Kane
* *Night of the Wolverine,* Dave Graney and the Coral Snakes

STAY
Littomore Hotel, 19 Charlotte Street, Bathurst

EAT
Pantano's Bar and Grill, 73 William Street – where the racing drivers eat!

VISIT
The officially duel named Mount Panorama/Wahluu in a car. You have to drive around this racetrack to really get a feel for it. It's quite a spectacular view at the top. An obvious meeting place for the Wiradjuri people.

POINT OF INTEREST
The Bathurst war between the Wiradjuri and the British settlers ran for a year in 1824.

Bathurst crowds from the olden days, courtesy National Motor Racing Museum.

Wiradjuri country is huge, and Bathurst sits on the eastern edge of it. Bathurst itself is quite a big country town with a population of over 40,000. It's a place with a vast history, and I'm not going to attempt anything more than a superficial glimpse through the windscreen for the moment. Through this gritty window we see another unique slice of Australia. The Bathurst car and bike races loom large in Australian consciousness, but they were largely absent from my own as I grew up. Even though I was uninterested in car racing, I still knew something went on there every year. In the 'seventies, mainstream Australian culture was fairly monolithic, so I couldn't avoid it. I associated the Bathurst 500 race with cricket, it came out of the black and white TV and seemed to take a long time, and came with a lot of noise. There were characters like Brock and Moffat. The cars were Ford and Holden. And some kids really got into it.

So I approached Brad Owen, the Coordinator of the National Motor Racing Museum with some trepidation. The museum sits right next to the racetrack at the bottom of 'the mountain'. I told him I was writing about a road trip, but I wasn't a rev head. I wondered if Brad would see through me? I need not have worried. I found him a warm, pleasant character and an engaging speaker. I also began to feel interested in this race for the first time. We've heard Brad in earlier chapters talking about the zen of driving, but let's return to him for another dose of car culture, back to those battles on the mountain. Not between

Bathurst riots – the ladies toilet block is stormed!

cars, but people. Remember those Bathurst riots in the 'eighties? Fire, beer cans, rocks and some pretty intense looking spectators.

Brad Owen: The Easter motorbike races, certainly in the 'eighties were wild. There were barbed wire compounds for the police. Riots and everything. And there's some interesting stories around what the truth of the matter was. Whether it was put on for the media, or whether it was the motorbike riders coming in from out of town. One of the theories I have heard is that it was actually the locals who had a good way of blowing off steam and taking out their frustrations on the local police. They could do it under the cover of people from out of town and be more anonymous. The truth lies somewhere in the middle and I don't think we'll ever know.

It seems that the Bathurst racing museum isn't trying to rewrite history just yet, and doesn't avoid these ugly moments. After all, it's a racetrack that seems to be deliberately designed to maximise car crashes. The Mount Panorama/Wahluu racetrack was made in 1938, well before the days of OH&S, and would not pass any sort of safety test today. But that's the spirit of this race. It's dangerous and that is part of the pleasure.

Brad Owen: Every person that comes to the track who's watched the race on TV will say the same thing: 'I can't believe it's so steep.' There's lots of blind corners, the walls are really close. And I think you see over the years, the guys that have done this race a whole lot of times, they will still make mistakes. Most of the corners, you can't exactly see where the exit is going. The V8 super cars and GT 3 cars are going in excess of 170 kilometres an hour. As you go into the corners, there are blind crests. There's a crest on top of the skyline, when you go over that, the road literally disappears in front of you. So it's a bit of an exercise in faith.

A more peaceful family crowd at the Bathurst races in the 1960s.

In the olden days, spectators could just wander around the track.

This comment about faith led to an interesting turn in the discussion. And we talked about the inexplicable element in elite sport. It took us into a sphere that was almost religious. And this is exactly the position that elite sport has filled in our secular world. You only have to look at soccer players (or football as they call it elsewhere) entering stadiums, crossing themselves, looking to the heavens. The feverish crowds chanting. The religious ecstasy after a goal. The skill to get those goals is almost beyond belief. Now maybe it's hard to see anything spiritual in car racing, but Brad had me travelling with him at high speed down the mountain.

Brad Owen: I reckon probably the vast majority of race drivers would be able to do the job up to 85 or 90 per cent. But the difference between doing it at 90 per cent and being in the top one or two is that 'X'-factor. That ability that only the top guys have got and you can't really put your finger on it. Whether it's mechanical sympathy, whether it's just bravery, whether it's reflexes. All that sort of thing. It's not necessarily the young guys, there's some sort of sweet spot between enthusiasm and fearlessness, and also wisdom and experience. It's just an amazing thing. I think in any sport, when you see that, you know when you see it, but you can't quite exactly work out what's going on that makes the difference.

But the Bathurst race is not what it was, when I didn't follow it in the 'seventies. How can it be the same without Ford and Holden? They're gone. The last local Holden left the plant in Elizabeth, South Australia, in 2017. They only make spare parts in Australia now. What's there to race for? I asked Brad if it was possible to race in my Kia?

Brad Owen: Probably not in Supercars. In the different countries, you wonder. In Korea, do the Hyundai guys and the Kia guys fight each other metaphorically like the Holden–Ford guys? It's a really weird thing. I have had a little bit of exposure to some German brands. The Mercedes guys hate the BMW guys, like the Ford guys hated the Holden guys, it's really interesting. And it seems to be much less

My Kia pays homage to the mountain.

of a kind of national specific issue, than you might think growing up here.

Australia is indeed a changed place. Perhaps we are a little softer for letting the Holden–Ford rivalry drift away. They were questionably Australian cars in the first place, and seemed to owe a lot to their American origins. As per my recommendation earlier – I like both Kia and Hyundai. Let them live in peace, side by side.

And as we wipe off the grime on the windscreen at the local Shell station, we remember those people that have died in the races on the mountain. Not that many according to Brad. My research leads me to believe there's been eighteen, including two spectators. Considering the treacherous nature of this circuit – that magical 'X'-factor must hang around that mountain in a big way.

SCANDAL RADAR

A corrupt arrangement between a Bathurst Regional Council employee and a supplier got slightly out of hand between 2004 and 2009, when $1.4 million was paid on falsified invoices for supplies that were never delivered – 444 kilometres of road mesh that could have lined the Great Western Highway between Bathurst and Sydney – or wrapped around the Mount Panorama circuit seventy-one times. Kudos for the imagination to create a false invoice for such an extreme measure – which council anywhere in the world would need such a massive amount of road mesh? How we long for those days when stealing a few pens or a ream of paper from the stationery cabinet was deemed to be at the cutting edge of corruption.

ST ARNAUD: LOOK DOWN THAT LONESOME ROAD

DJA DJA WURRUNG COUNTRY

MUSIC
* *Release The Bats*, the Birthday Party
* *No Fun*, the Stooges
* *Lonesome Road*, Gene Austin

STAY
La Cochon Rose, 123 Napier Street, St Arnaud

EAT
Country Kitchen – all day.
Country Delights – breakfast and lunch.
Royal Hotel – lunch and dinner.

VISIT
St Arnaud Books, the home of Australian Literature

RANDOM POINT OF INTEREST
Nick Cave wandered the fields of nearby Warracknabeal as a very young child – although he left there at the age of two! It would seem that it made him introspective and angry, or maybe that was just Caulfield Grammar School.

And so we travel down that lonesome road. To be specific we're on the Wimmera Highway, the B240, in central Victoria. It's a magnificent, goldy wheaty, rural experience, with the Grampian Mountains hovering on the horizon nearby. St Arnaud is a small town of around 2,000 people and a fairly random choice of destination. But the reason I'm coming here is to visit Gus, the singer from my very early punk band in Canberra, Guthugga Pipeline. I expanded on this fascinating musical ensemble at the start of the book. He has chosen to live here in semi-retirement with his partner Jane, and set up a book shop of all things, devoted to Australian literature of all things! In the smallest of towns. A niche within a niche within a niche. But this is all part of our journey dear drivers. To seek the things that make the journey of life a kaleidoscope of experience. You don't have to go to Paris to rifle through books by exotic authors that no one remembers.

Gavin 'Gus' Butler: Australian books only. Literature, poetry and history. The reason we could do it here was because the rents are so cheap. To put it bluntly, you could never do it in a city.

It is very odd to find yourself transcribing your childhood friend's dialogue. Me and Gus were in kindergarten together, learning how to spell! And while I've been writing this work and hopefully getting the spelling roughly correct (courtesy various software). I realise it's partly a search for some sort of 'authentic' Australian. Right next door to Gus's house lives a perfect specimen. David Hines is an octogenarian farmer, with a passion for banjos. While me and Gus were making our own fun with a dodgy punk band in Canberra, he had forged the way ahead many years before. Out in the Australian countryside in the 1950s. Dave was truly in a world of his own.

David Hines: In the country you have to make things happen and if something breaks down you fix it whether it's wire or string. I didn't have a nice banjo so I made one. School wasn't my favourite place and

During his long life, David has rarely travelled far from St Arnaud.

you're in the presence of one, you don't feel confused.

David Hines: I just thought you could probably interview somebody a bit more interesting. I'm a farmer not legally retired yet, but my neighbours haven't seen me do much lately. But I've had a great life with the animals and music and I've been very fortunate to miss all the wars. If they don't destroy your arms and legs, they destroy your head. So I've been very fortunate.

The wider local region also has some confusing historical elements. Having studied in the school of punk rock, Gus was aware that just down the road a more successful Australian punk had wandered (or perhaps crawled) through misty fields. Warracknabeal, just down the Sunraysia Highway (B220), is the birthplace of Nick Cave! That's what the town claims anyway, and a larger than life size statue of Nick Cave on a horse is being planned as I write.

I left. It was a dry year and we had a family farm with a lot of sheep on it and no grass. So I was sent off, out to the long paddock up the road, with a mob of sheep. We converted an old buggy into a covered wagon like a gypsy van and a horse. And I took an old banjo and three dogs. Sixty-five years later I've got eight dogs and eight banjos, so that's a success story for you!... My wife calls me Vasco de Gama the big traveller. I shifted bedrooms once in fifty years so you know I'm not all that worldly.

But moving from one side of the house to the other can be a journey in itself. Depends what happens in the bedroom, or inside the traveller. In my brief encounter, I found David an uplifting character. The best of the old Australia. These people are disappearing and now represent our somewhat foggy national history. But when

I checked the facts with rock writer Clinton Walker, who coincidentally happened to have lived in these parts as a child. He's also spent time with Nick Cave in the junkie brotherhood.

Clinton Walker, punk rock writer:
Warracknabeal is not very far from where I was growing up at the same time in the late 1950s, and it's not as if we've ever really compared notes on that. I can only imagine that life for Nick Cave was not dissimilar. We lived on the edge of Bendigo. So you're sort of on the edge of town. It's really paddocks at the back of the house. I just ran around. My sister almost drowned in a stormwater drain, that was the sort of thing we did. Bendigo was full of old gold mines. So if you leaned over too far, that's the last we see of you.

Because we are an international publication we can make light of Nick Cave's childhood exploits, but in Victoria you must be very careful. Especially in Melbourne, around that central ring of suburbs. His legend is growing old, but it still causes occasional rapture and keeps the second hand suit economy hot.

Clinton Walker: In Sydney, you can't make fun of Jimmy Barnes, in Brisbane, you can't make fun of Ed Kuepper or Robert Forster. I tend to find that with Nick Cave, you get extremes. You will meet some people who go – he's a god! Please make another film about him. Write another book about him...please. And then other people go – who?

David Hines, St Arnaud's banjo playing, octogenarian farmer, is one of these kind.

David Hines: I actually didn't know he was born up here. He's not my sort of music. But our daughter is a music therapist and she was going to homes to visit old people and one of them was Nick Cave's mother. And she was a bit of a hoot. So that's how I knew of his name.

Music therapy. It's what all we musicians were unwittingly doing before it had a name. I wonder what effect 'Release the Bats' would have on Nick Cave's mother. It may work in the same way that electroshock therapy does. And all over Australia in the 'eighties, there were bands attempting this kind of cure. Me and Gus were a lot less successful than Nick Cave, when it came to delivering the medicine. But we learned about it the same way, from our colonial masters in the UK.

> **Gus:** There was this five-minute show on TV, *Weekend Panorama* (a BBC program). I guess it was in 1977. And it showed the Sex Pistols for five minutes. And I just thought that's the most bizarre thing I've ever seen. I was totally enraptured by this completely extraordinary band.

As a country that mobbed visiting royalty, Australia back in the 'seventies was much more British than it appears now. Although I would qualify that by saying the Queen is still immensely popular. Australia's literature (as in books) has its roots strongly planted in the old country. As a wandering country lad, Nick Cave probably read the same books that me and Gus did. Biggles anyone?

> **Clinton Walker**: Almost certainly one thing I would have had in common with Nick Cave in those days is that he was a reader. And this is something that happened to me. I think there's more of a culture of reading in country areas to this day. We didn't have TV. I was into books, and I've become a writer. And it was just something I loved from the very first and it was something that would take you away. I was certainly reading Imperial literature, adventure stories, Robert Louis Stevenson, H.G. Wells and these kinds of things. And when you get into that, it takes your head somewhere very different. And I learned to love that really young and so did Nick Cave. I mean, his father was a school teacher. So he was possibly getting some guidance there.

Gus tells me that rural crime is the biggest seller in their bookshop. That's a novel where an unlikely murder occurs out in the fields, and various characters are suspected in a long drawn out plot, with plenty of lavish descriptions of scenery and eccentric country folk. In our story the chief suspect would be David Hines. We recall that he has access to a lot of wire. And why did he change bedrooms suddenly? But perhaps the deceased really did just trip and fall down an old gold mine, scramble out and stumble against a barbed wire fence, and collapse in a field. Just like David tells Beck O'Reilly, the long serving cantankerous country cop. Bullshit! She's heard it all before.

'How long have I known you for Davo?'

If you've read this far, you'll have come across some of my own early attempts at creative writing. It's quite possible that you skipped over them. Don't feel guilty. We all have very short attention spans these days. But there was a time when I delved into Australia's authors, David Ireland springs to mind. *The Glass Canoe*, 1976. I don't think that book would pass the cancel culture mob test anymore.[41] It came out in that 'seventies period, when there was an infor-

---

41 One Australian writer who's had a nasty time with the online kangaroo court is Clinton Walker.

mal Australian arts movement underway. Some of it would appear naive today. But at least people were giving it a go. *Don's Party*, a play then a film. *Alvin Purple*, a silly but extremely popular film. *Dimboola*! A play about a wedding at a town, just a bit further away from St Arnaud than Warracknabeal. The Wimmera region is indeed a cultural hub like no other.

Clinton Walker: As I got older, I started to read a lot more Australian literature, probably for historical reasons as much as anything else. In the early 'eighties, my mind was turned by contemporary literature, and it was turned by three writers Helen Garner, Robert Drew, and Peter Corris. Peter Corris wrote hardball detective stories set in Sydney. I love noir crime fiction. So I love seeing Cliff Hardy, his detective, grow through that series. Helen Garner was chronicling the Melbourne druggie underground, and I liked that too. And Robert Drew wrote a great collection of short stories called *The Bodysurfers*.

Get down to St Arnaud Australian bookshop and get hold of some of this material. Before it disappears into the ether.

Eddy Jokovich, New Politics: I can recall a futurist talking about books twenty years ago, and his suggestion was that with ebooks and different forms of publishing, the book wouldn't exist anymore. Twenty years ago! They've been around for such a long, long time. And more people are reading more books today – they might be reading ebooks, they might be reading printed books, but they're still reading books. This idea of the printed book disappearing completely – that hasn't turned out to be true.

To me it's such a relief to get off the ubiquitous screens and read something at the end of the day. Just like you're doing now. Although you can still relax if you are reading it as an ebook. Just by zoning out with some connected text you are extending your life! True. Like the zone we dip in and out of, on our road trip. So as we leave St Arnaud and drive on, we leave David Hines with his banjos and dogs, strumming a clean, clear version of 'Lonesome Road'.

Look down, look down, that lonesome road
Before you travel on
Look up, look up and greet your maker,
before Gabriel blows his horn.

Barkly Street, Footscray

Wurundjeri Woi Wurrung and Bunurong Country

MUSIC
* *Ajak Kwai* – Nasalah Belletna made this clip and all. Check it out on Greg Appel's YouTube channel
* *Romper Stomper Theme*, John Clifford White

STAY
The Footscray Hotel, looks pretty good to me, a bargain.

EAT
Footscray Market

VISIT
You can't go past Betta electrical store where Alice Pung's family have a big range of screens, fans, musical instruments and much much more.

RANDOM POINT OF INTEREST
Harry's Shoes Plus at 235 Barkly Street has been a shoe store since 1956. When they branched out into prison uniforms and women's lingerie to keep the business afloat, Harry added the 'Plus'.

You get a good view of Melbourne as you come into town on a few different routes. It's a cityscape that's changed a lot since I first drove down here. Some buildings have sprouted cow patches while others look like Soviet-era cubist hybrids. Then the shiny Eureka Tower pokes upwards through it all. There's definitely something going on with the architecture that Sydney isn't quite doing.

When I used to come here with bands, I really only knew one road. Punt Road. It seemed to always go from anywhere you were, to anywhere you'd want to go. It was also one of the few roads with a hill so you could see where you actually were. Melbourne is quite a flat place. And much of the time you can feel a little lost amongst the grid layout and the trams.

As far as traffic speed goes, it wins the prize of the slowest Australian city to my knowledge. That's not to say it's without its charms. The trams themselves are great. All the cities have had trams, then got rid of them and often come back with them again – in the form of light rail. Frivolous Sydney even went monorail for a while. But once the city council saw *The Simpsons* episode featuring a monorail, its days were numbered. Usually, Australia's bigger cities regret getting rid of trams, and wily

Melbourne writer, Alice Pung and Celeste at the Beta Electrical Store.

old Melbourne never did. Five stars for wisdom.

Sydney and Melbourne have a kind of quantum entanglement, especially the inner cities, that have exchanged populations over the years. COVID has strained this relationship, but let's put that behind. Despite their slightly more serious way of seeing the world, despite their more formal dress code, Melbourne is a marvelous place. And over the years I've learned that it's a lot of different marvelous places. It's a very segmented city. Footscray was an area of Melbourne I knew little about 'til recently. I knew they had a football team and that was about it.

To some, Melbourne is the 'it' city. European. Cosmopolitan. Very stylish. A wonderland even. That's how Kuan Pung, the father of Alice Pung, the Melbourne writer, found it. He was a refugee from Pol Pot's killing fields who ended up at the Midway Migrant Hostel down the road from Footscray. That's where Alice was born, named after *Alice in Wonderland*, the Chinese language version was Kuan's favourite book. I met Kuan through Alice, and had the pleasure of buying a very reasonably priced fan from the family store, Betta electrical. I had to admit to all concerned that I had a neurotic disorder and needed white noise to sleep. Fans have always helped this problem.

Alice Pung: I grew up in this shop after school. Instead of going home to watch *Captain Planet* on one television, we'd watch it on twenty. Sometimes, we'd be joined by the children of customers, and they'd squeal when they were dragged away. As we grew older, we became sales assistants with our own name tags, and our personalities were pared down to one line. How can I help you? Other kids at school had the holiday season, but in our world, there were only three seasons: pre-sale, sale and stock-take.

I was in the electrical shop to make another radio program about a street. Alice Pung would be the guide to Barkly Street. She is a writer who would never write 'Soviet-era cubist hybrids' like I did a few paragraphs ago. I don't know what came over me, maybe I had a pretentious panic attack induced by the Melbourne skyline appearing from way down Sydney Road. Alice has a straightforward easy-to-read style that has won her prizes and a much bigger reading audience than poor old architecturally-threatened me.

Alice Pung: My mother can't speak English very well. She can't read or write either. So I think my style is relatively simple. And I get it from translating for parents or explaining a world that they weren't born into from a

very young age. I was published when I was relatively young. My first book came out when I was twenty-five. I didn't understand very much about class, because I'd grown up around the streets of Footscray. It was a very disorientating experience, because many writers come from a certain middle class background. Because that's how you get time to write. You've got a steady job, or you've got, parental support. So it's been interesting. But it's been a great thing, because I've always been able to work around noise, in very confined spaces at the back of a shop, in a room that we shared with two other siblings. So writing is a privilege to me.

We chose to make a program about Footscray because? I never could quite remember, but working with Melbourne producer Frances Green, who we met earlier as a hitchhiker and Joburg-style driver, was definitely part of it. It proved to be exactly the right choice. It reminded me of *King Street, Newtown*, the original TV program about a street I'd made with Steve Brown way back in 1995. Similar vibe but different too. That edge of gentrification.

Alice Pung: Footscray has traditionally been a working class area. Money was hard to come by. At our shop – there was a man with a watering can who went around watering the money trees near the front doors of the stores so that the businesses would thrive. We always gave him a tip.

That's how Alice writes, clear and direct. So let's put an hour on the parking meter and take a short walk down this amazing street with her.

and more recently, South Sudan. All places that had experienced conflict. And now it's being transformed again, with high rise apartments and gentrification, and a new wave of hipsters to add to the mix. But it's that Melbourne form of football, AFL, that seems to bind the community together. The Western Bulldogs home ground is on Barkly Street.

Susan Alberti, AC: When you sit there in the grandstand, looking back towards the city, you feel like you could almost touch those buildings. It's an incredible sight. And then you look to the side and you look at the West Gate Bridge, you see all the cars going over there. It's a hub of activity on Barkly Street.

Since I'm not super familiar with Footscray, it might be best to let the locals speak for themselves.

Richard Treagar, social worker: They spent hundreds of millions of dollars policing Barkly Street and the surroundings with forty cameras. But what really changed it was that people realised that Barkly Street and Footscray were incredibly beautiful.

Harry Rafalowicz, Harry's Shoe Store: If you don't look for trouble, it's not going to find you. And if you want to walk into the lion's den, then don't be upset if you get bitten.

Grant Miles, former Mayor, owner of 'Cheaper by Miles': The great thing about Footscray is that it's a suburb that is based around small businesses. There's no McDonald's here. There's no KFC here. It keeps that circular economy going.

Perched on a band in the Maribyrnong River, in Melbourne's western suburbs, Footscray has a reputation, it was the centre of a heroin epidemic in the 'nineties and featured in the film *Romper Stomper*, where Russell Crowe, played an Asian-bashing neo-Nazi. The suburb has absorbed waves of immigration over the last century, from Greece and Italy after the second world war, then Vietnam in the 'seventies and 'eighties

Alice Pung: I was practically raised on Barkly Street. I was wandering the streets by myself, when I was about eleven. My earliest memory of Barkly Street would have been when I was about four with my grandmother, who was the oldest surviving person in her collective in Pol Pot's killing fields. There were 5,000 people in that collective, she was the only old person who emerged alive. And when she came to Australia, she was in her seventies. And Australia gave her twenty more years of life, which meant she lived far longer than most of my cousins who perished in that regime. And so she was very close to me. We shared the same bed, and she would walk down Barkly Street with a walking stick. She was very Buddhist. If she saw rubbish, she would poke it with her walking stick, which might have had a little pin on the end or something. I don't know how she magically picked up chip packets and things like that. And she would put them in bins. And when I was small, I thought she was the best grandmother ever. But as I got older, I was a bit embarrassed about this, you know, rubbish-picking-up grandmother.

As we walked around, we kept coming back to the Western Bulldogs AFL team.

I don't think it's a big deal. If you didn't go for the Bulldogs, you'd probably feel a bit adrift amongst this sea of red, white and blue. But the reason I go for the Bulldogs is because we went to a primary school in the western suburbs, and every month without fail, the Bulldogs would come and give the kids breakfast. And we felt so special. These tall footballers, coming to give us breakfast. And boys would bring their footy cards for the footballers to sign. It was only as an adult that I realised we were one of the most disadvantaged schools in Victoria and the Bulldogs did this as part of community service. They never let us know that we were the povo kids that they came to bestow their magnificent benevolence upon.

At the back of Alice's fathers electrical shop, we came up on a mural of a bulldog decked out in red, white and blue, cocking its leg in that familiar position. It turned out to be an artwork created by Kevin Rudd's artistic nephew. And it had caused a bit of excitement in the media when it was first sprayed on the wall. That man cannot stay away from publicity! Even via his brother's son.

trical too! But the local council wasn't too keen on the attention.

Alice Pung: The following day, it was all painted over so you can't see Pauline Hanson's face. But they didn't dare paint over the Bulldog because the council knew if you painted over the icon of the west, there would be big trouble.

Van Rudd: It was almost like the council had an artistic input like they've edited it, you know going, maybe we can make it better.

There's been generations of artists that have been attracted to the area. Neil Taylor, a metal sculptor, takes inspiration from local industrial history.

Van Rudd: I consider myself an art student forever. My mother came out of Vietnam during the war around 1971. And she'd met my father in Vietnam during the war. He was an Australian soldier. So at that time, it was about 2017. It was a time period where the far right was in a sort of resurgent mode. So I was itching to do something out there in protest, I was really negative when I went out there, I thought, I'm never gonna find a wall. No one's gonna support me. And lo and behold, I walked into an electrical store.

Kuan Pung, Betta electrical store:
There's a guy, he asked me whether you can paint anything (on the wall).

So Alice's father Kuan, let Van Rudd paint on his shop's back wall. It turned out to be a large mural of a Bulldog pissing on Pauline Hanson's head. The next day all the news channels turned up, and Kuan wondered what all the fuss was about. Alice explained, and Kuan thought it was pretty funny. Good publicity for Beta Elec-

The first Chemist Warehouse in Australia is on Barkly Street! Info source: Alice Pung.

Neil Taylor: As a friend of mine says 'You're living on the wrong side of the wrong river.' It's just really nice to have Footscray at your fingertips, it's a very pleasant place to be. The street constantly changes. But it's always commerce at that sort of slightly low level suburban shopping strip. A shop will die and something else will take its place. And within three or four months, it's totally obliterated the memory of what was there. But what is interesting is that if you look up above the verandas, all the facades are pretty much original. All Victorian and stuff from the 1920s and 'thirties. So you can take a little historical walk down there and just look up.

Back in the car, we'll switch on Ajak Kwai, to get the sounds of the wave of migrants from the Horn of Africa, fused with a bit of a Footscray jive. Ajak is someone I've worked with a number of times. She has had quite a life, from running around with goats as a young girl in South Sudan, to a refugee camp in Egypt, to Hobart, to Melbourne.

Ajak Kwai: We had a civil war going on for more than forty years. So when I left Sudan I was very sad because it was such a beautiful place. Footscray is the only place I could go to the shop. There's no security following you around. And that is a good feeling.

But when asked, Ajak will also talk about the worst aspects of Australian behaviour. Being yelled at and spat on in the street. Really unpleasant stories.

Ajak Kwai: I would never call Australia racist country because there are more good people in Australia than those who make our life hell. And a lot of South Sudanese are pushed out of Footscray because it's become quite expensive. So we go to a suburb very far away and it's harder for us to visit one another.

As we drive out of Melbourne towards the M80 ring road we pass the suburb of Sunshine, one of the suburbs where the South Sudanese diaspora now live. It's a lovely name for another suburban place. But the multicultural mix of people and factories seems very familiar. It recalls the early days of Footscray but with more space.

A sprawling mass of houses, trees and yards broken by industrial shapes and shopping centres. When cars took over the world in the 'sixties it allowed people to commute just that bit further and live the quarter acre dream. The name Sunshine hints at this. It goes all the way back to the start of the nineteenth century when the first factory was set up on Sunshine Estate, with the idea that workers could live nearby. Today, it often appears on commercial channel news stories about African gangs. Perhaps the time has come for gentrifying these ring suburbs as people flee the close confines of the inner city. Looking for fresh air and social distance. Will gentrification come to Sunshine? Or will it drift into decay.

SCANDAL RADAR

Aside from being a cultural hub of Melbourne, Australian rules football is an integral part of Footscray's identity. But way before match fixing became a 'thing' in professional sport, Port Melbourne players were offered £100 bribes – from Port Melbourne players! – to 'play dead' in the 1922 VFA Grand Final and fix the result in Footscray's favour. They refused and went on to win the match by two points, their integrity intact, if not a little poorer. The players involved were given life bans.

Sections of this chapter can be heard on the *Earshot* documentary, 'Greetings from Footscray', ABC Radio National – abc.net.au/rn

THE SUNSHINE STATE

> **MUSIC**
> * *Swing for the Crime*, the Saints
> * *The Bitch is Back*, Elton John
> * *Treat You Right*, the Jungle Giants
> * *Head Full of Steam*, the Go-Betweens
>
> **STAY**
> Madison Tower Mill Hotel, 239 Wickham Terrace, Brisbane City
>
> **EAT**
> Red Hook – an excellent burger bar, 3/88 Creek Street, Brisbane
>
> **VISIT**
> Queensland Gallery of Modern Art, Stanley Place, South Brisbane
>
> **RANDOM POINT OF INTEREST**
> If you get sick of the art at QAGOMA, you can hire the futuristic electric scooters nearby.

And now to the real sunshine. Queensland is a place I mainly know through holidays and elections. It always gets noticeably more tropical as you cross the border from NSW. The palm trees multiply, people wearing thongs and tropical shirts emerge from behind every hibiscus. Brisbane might be a more modern city that it was back in the Bjelke–Petersen era but it still seems hot and muggy and in need of a closer beach. Indeed, the Gold Coast is pretty much the first thing we pass as we pelt along the double-laned freeway on Highway 1. It's an Australian ode to Florida – enough said. I remember when dad took us there for a family holiday, we asked to go somewhere else. What a bunch of spoiled brats.

YUGAMBEH AND TURRBAL COUNTRY (GOLD COAST AND BRISBANE)

The Gold Coast, Sunshine Coast and Brisbane sometimes get joined up and called Brisvegas these days. It can have that feel. Elvis would be at home here. When I think of all the road trips we did as kids. Unseatbelted in the back of a station wagon. The one that brings the strongest essence of nostalgia was to Tangalooma, on Moreton Island, in Moreton Bay, not so very far from Brisbane.

We had to travel all the way from frigid Canberra. My father reminded me that this wasn't the kind of trip you got up early for, you went in the afternoon. It was an overnighter. Free accommodation for the whole family as we lay down in a row at the back of the car or across seats. With five kids that was a lot of potential projectiles. But dad would forge into the night. I remember the light changing and looking up at the trees and wires as we hurtled along before being rocked into a deep sleep. There must have been many families speeding around at night like this.

> **Clinton Walker:** I remember crashing on the run to Brisbane. My sisters screaming, blood everywhere, the ambulance sirens. My mother was hysterical. My father's head was hanging through the driver's side window, which was half open and now smashed. There was blood everywhere. I thought he was dead and it's a wonder we didn't die.

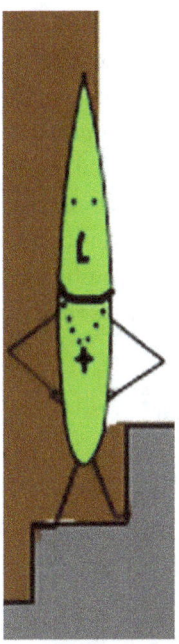

Even though the roads were bad, and we drove all night – I don't remember any accidents. Providence was with us as they used to say. Being the oldest I took charge of entertainment in the back. This was where stories like 'The Little Thing' were recounted. I won't inflict this one on you, but the core of the story was that the Little Thing could never be described. It just did things. Sometimes my siblings would try and describe it, but I would assure them this was not possible. There was also 'Clean Bean'. Much easier to describe his thin green bean-like body.

He has lived on, into my own children's world. He has a camp theatrical voice and loves cleaning up. This may sound dull but that bean has had some wild adventures. His foe Dirty Burt is always ready to spread filth if there are any gaps in the plot.

The Little Thing and Clean Bean may have even been friends once. This tale waits for Marvel to approach me for an all-in-one block buster.[42]

We drove all the way to Brisbane to get to Tangalooma. Brisbane is just the start of Queensland of course, and an urban version. Still it's got quite a different feel to the other Australian cities. It's all steamy and tropical and feels a bit heat stroked. It's got a mad history too. Joh Bjelke–Petersen, the longest serving state Premier for Queensland from 1968 to 1987, ruled over this kingdom for much of my young life. There even seems to be a branch of my family that is related to the Petersens. I dare not research it.

Clinton Walker: You had to hand it to Joh Bjelke–Petersen. Like one of his big inspirations, Adolf Hitler, he was really good at building freeways. To get from Tweed Heads up to Brisbane in the old days, it would take three or more hours, and it's not even 100 miles. The 'Magnolia Curtain' was an expression they used to use for the Mason–Dixon line in the US when you went down south. I called this the 'Pineapple Curtain'. I'd never seen a pineapple in 1969 when I moved there. What is that? An avocado. What is that? Queensland was just full of tropical fruit. There wasn't that much difference between NSW and Victoria, but Queensland!

Queensland was a true banana republic, and in some ways has remained a state unto itself. A heady mix of corruption, out of control police and sweaty madness. There were many refugees from this regime that found their way down South when I lived in Sydney in the 1980s. They would tell stories of the city and sing and dance about it. There were some great bands that came from up there during this period. The Saints of course were a big part of my early listening. I don't know if I ever purchased any Saints records, in fact I went out of my way to purchase as few records as I could. Other peoples' records and a handy cassette machine were my main way of keeping up with new music. Yes, piracy, copyright infringement and ripping off musos has been

---

42 The Clean Bean idea could be more universal than I originally suspected. In the British Series *Black Books* there is a distinctly bean like character that makes an appearance. Check the episode 'Grapes of Wrath'. Great show anyway.

going on for eons. Although it's debatable whether paying for a record ever meant that money went into those surly looking Saints pockets. However I heard it, the Saints' last album *Prehistoric Sounds* is embedded in my psyche. Some amazing tracks on this record. Let's put one on for the Queensland journey. 'Swing for the Crime', 1978. Not quite sure what it's about, but it fits the state, the era and we like it.

Clinton Walker: When I first got to Queensland, I was beaten up by the police and everybody I knew was beaten up. This is what happened to you in Brisbane in the 1970s. If you ever went on a protest march – that was illegal – so you'd get beaten up and hauled away. The police were still wearing brown uniforms, and I used to think they looked like the brown shirts. It's really hard to convey how bizarre and oppressive Queensland was and why it produced that music and bands that it produced then. A blazing punk band, like the Saints, then the next big band that comes out of Brisbane, is the Go-Betweens. They could not be more different, the Saints were loud, fast, aggressive, and raw. And the Go-Betweens were fey, plodding, they couldn't play – very poetic, very arty. But in some ways, I totally hear Brisbane in both of those bands. Neither of those bands could have come from Melbourne or Sydney.

The scene in Brisbane sounded very similar to the one I had grown up with in Canberra. There was nothing on, so you had to make your own fun. If you can call punk fun. So some classic Australian music might have been forged in this muggy atmosphere.

But what went on in Brisbane at the time, was a long way from my middle class travel experience. We were like many Australian families, oblivious and asleep to any of the darker undercurrents below the surface of our northern paradise.

And so our holiday drives to Brisbane were all about avoiding the city. The streets seemed permanently on the verge of melting. What better way to skip over any of that hot dark stuff than by getting out of the car, shuffling across a tarmac, and boarding a light aircraft. I should have been more nervous at the time, but I was just a child on the brink of adolescence. That should have made me nervous too!

TANGALOOMA: NGUGI COUNTRY

The island holiday experience of the 'seventies was something else. Australia itself is a large island and remains largely invisible to the rest of the world. But an island off an island, that's where you can really make a little paradise. I'm not sure why the surrounding seas and feeling of being in another dimension made these places so desirable, but Tangalooma was paradise to me. The *kitsch* travel brochures don't really do it justice.

The climate of Moreton Island, where Tangalooma was nestled, was very pleasant compared to hot and cold Canberra where we came from. People were a lot friendlier too. We made family friends on the plane that would last for life. Every day there were new friends. It was like one of those British holiday camps, minus the drizzle and whinging poms. I guess these island retreats were modelled on British holiday camps, but here they had a new meaning. My explanation for this pleasurable life

There was something about those Queensland travel brochures that made me collect them as a young boy.

will sound pretty un-exiting now, but I'll try. The world has changed and on top of having a vague guilty feeling for my privileged young self, there's the layers of age that encrust the mind, making it difficult to see through a child's eyes.

Pool tables and the exciting semi criminal element of getting a 20-cent piece attached to a fishing line to get infinity free games. There must have been an adult involved here to drill a hole in the 20-cent piece, but it made pool so much more fun. The possibility of romance. Always in the warm air. I think of those pre-sexual crushes as true romances. Never really requited but truly meaningful and incredibly exciting. Plastic dolphin shaped drink stirring things. Amazingly indulgent tools for those pink lemonades that hinted at an adult life to come, without requiring any of the effort of being one.

Fishing for hours on the jetty. No guilt about pulling up many inedible 'butter-bream' that were put in a bucket to thrash out the last of their lives. And the sea of course. Always there, nice and calm and clear on the Tangalooma side. Wild and rough, but quite interesting on the other side of the island, where you could travel in an ex army duck to gaze and wonder. Another short trip was 'the wrecks' a stack of old ships that were left to rust, and had now become ecosystems full of exotic fish. Which brings me to the present era.

It so happens that I did revisit my childhood dream resort, courtesy of a cruise ship in 2016. The type of cheap crowded voyage that the pre-COVID era was all about. The trip itself was fine. While there was a touch of the floating RSL about it, once you got past that – it was very good value for money. That's if disease wasn't an issue. Anyway, once we got to Moreton Island, the tenders[43] were crammed full of people and lowered overboard. We landed at Tangalooma like it was D-Day. It was completely destroyed. Where once a small and charmingly dilapidated resort had stood, was now a series of ugly modern buildings that could dispense all the crap required by an army of cruislings. Oh well – you can't stop progress. The wrecks were still pretty good. Maybe better, as more fish had moved in and it had become quite the tropical reef.

I was of course ignorant of the origins of the name Tangalooma as a child. It sounded like a badly made up name for an island resort. I now learn by that internationally recognised font of all knowledge – the internet – that Tangalooma is an Indigenous location name, meaning 'where the fish gather.' And they certainly do.

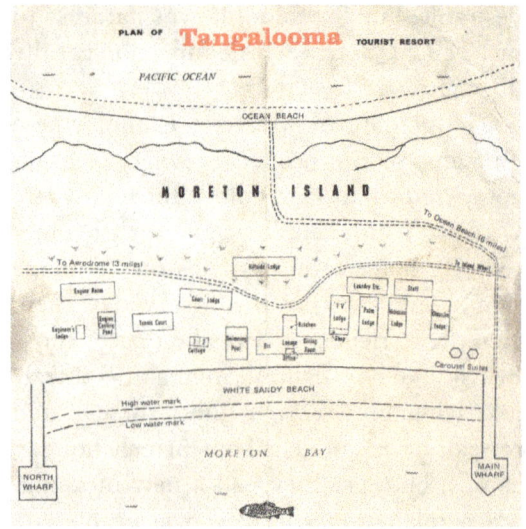

43 Dinghies.

Back at the Wrecks, 2016. I seem to be doing a 'piece to camera' for some reason.

MALENY: NALBO AND DALLAMBARA COUNTRY

This brings me to another trip to Queensland, I made this one in the mid-nineties. It's a darker anecdote, and I struggle to get the tone right. I often wondered whether you could use documentary evidence to arrest people for admitting to crimes in the past. Like I've wondered about how old rockers can continually write in books about how many illegal drugs they consumed, without policemen knocking at the door.

Anyway, we're off to the beautiful little gentrified town of Maleny. It's a very pleasant short drive north of Brisbane, up the M1, turn left onto Steve Irwin Way and then left again at Landsborough, up through the Glasshouse Mountains. In this picturesque setting I had my most terrifying experience as a documentary maker. Media people might talk tough, but like the punks from Canberra in my youth, I found that they were often nervous of any confrontation, either verbal or physical. It was often the cause of long re-edits when people didn't say what they thought in the first place, and no one would say who was in charge as that was too…confrontational. I was made of exactly the same stuff.

Myself and an ABC TV News editor called Steve Brown had made a documentary about King Street in Newtown, with a gang of fellow ABC News workers. We'd sold this documentary back to the ABC, who perhaps should have just deducted that payment from our regular wages. It had then become a big success. A big success for an ABC documentary anyway. So now we were making the follow up.

We carefully worked on the formula for

A BEAT POEM
by Wayne McAllister

Landscape desisting in the rearview mirror
a 52 floor stiffy
built by politicians, property developers
and a terribly excited architect
monuments to business acumen
purveyors of the modern conditions disappear
to the bogong moths on the windshield,
and the radiator grille.
I see the smudged milkers
black and white, black and white

Yeah. He's talking about cows man! Bernard King and his friend Simpilcio, who was happy to play the chauffeur in full uniform, pulled up in their hire car.

Beat poet Wayne, hops in and we find ourselves in Maleny, with an electric cast of characters. Including Peg Burnett, a resident of eighty years, Melissa Lloyd, who gave a birth on camera on the same plot of earth the baby was conceived on, Eve Fesl, a Gubbi Gubbi elder and Paul Alister, a member of the Ananda Marga, who'd been arrested for the Hilton Bombing in 1979 then acquitted eleven years later. If the Hilton Bombing means anything to you, you will know that conspiracy theories have been around long before the internet. This program was made just as the whole connected thing was beginning to gain traction with Netscape. What a wonderful world was coming!

The people in Maleny were friendly, open and giving, just like they've been on all the street programs I've been involved with. Why people trust a bunch of strangers to edit their intimate thoughts into entertainment I will

the next part. Newtown in the countryside. Hippies and farmers. Indigenous and settlers. A star. Bernard King, the famous camp cook from 1960s' TV, had grown up there and agreed to partake. We had our lucky mascot, our Newtown doco host, Wayne McCallister, who was another creative ABC editor and sometime poet. In fact he came up with a groundbreaking beat poem that opened the program over a Brisbane/rural montage, as a thought track.

never really know. But I am indebted to them.

There was actually an ABC *7.30* report guy in town, who thought we were more of a current affairs program than we were. He gave us a lot of contacts from the Bunya trading side of town. These were a group of people who were starting their own currency called Bunya, named after the local Bunya tree. It allowed them to barter goods amongst their like minded friends. Again, Bitcoin is not really a new phenomena, it's just got the entire internet behind it.

People from the less progressively minded community in town thought of the Bunya traders as greeny ratbags. We thought the kind of people who might think this were underrepresented in our program. So we put the word out for some 'colourful characters'. I don't know who gave us Big Jim Doyle's address. But perhaps they should have warned us.

The stench was strong from quite a long distance away. As we drove down the dirt road, the howls and barks of dogs were the next thing that we noticed. We could see dead animal carcasses all around the house. They were the main reason for the strong smell. The dogs did not seem friendly. Big Jim was quick to come to the door. Suitably dressed for television in his baggy shorts and nothing else. He was ready for the camera straight away.

Jim Doyle: I never did like Maleny. We used to call them inbreds from right the way back. They're cunts and they've never been anywhere.

Then he started ranting about a couple of bushwalkers who accidentally walked onto his property.

Jim Doyle: I'll give you a bushwalking. You'll finish up with three eyes. I said 'your mates will find you as a heap of dog shit under that shady tree over there.' They both started howling and crying and screaming. They thought they were gonna get murdered. Ha ha ha. Anyway, I said tell your, dole bulging, marijuana chewing mates to keep up off my bloody land.

I was doing duty as a sound recordist at that point, I looked at Steve and Mike, the camera guy, as if to say, 'I think we've got it all! Let's get out of here!' They looked back with the same nervous expression. But no! Big Jim had other plans for us. Camera rolling and furry mic pointed at him, we went into his house. He wanted to show us something. He pointed to a photo

Jim Doyle: Can you get this? That's my old man. He lived 'til he was ninety-two, Dagger Doyle. And that's my mother and father there and their golden wedding anniversary. She had fourteen kids. Seven boys, seven girls.

We went further in. It was a very well dressed set. Straight from a horror film. Stuff everywhere, the stench overwhelming. Jim pulled open drawers in his bedside table and produced a huge gun which he casually pointed everywhere. We were now truly terrified.

Jim Doyle: That's what I shot blacks with. That's a Smith and Weston 38.

We got out of there as fast as we could. The program went to air on the ABC in 1996. There were some complaints, but nothing happened to Jim Doyle to my knowledge.

NAMBOUR: KABI KABI COUNTRY

Think back to my earlier idea about going to 5-star rated places that no one goes to and taking a detour to visit places nearby. Then double the stars and divide by 10, then subtract one. Nambour is a town with no rating. You drive from Maleny by the very scenic Highway 23 take a few turns and you're there. Kind of near Noosa Heads (5-stars) on the Sunshine Coast but not really on the coast. However, it's definitely a place worth visiting in my book. It was another kind of documentary that sent me to Nambour. Long after the days when Big Jim Doyle was broadcast in 4-by-3 aspect off SP Betcam tape to bewildered audiences on ABC TV, I came across a podcast made by the people of Nambour. About their town.

"Nambour, it's got McDonald's too!"

For better or worse, podcasting has made every conversation into something broadcastable. There's now, an incredible din of people talking to each other, criss-crossing the world. But like everything on the internet, amongst all this noise are some moments of pure gold. Technology had reached this semi-country town. Once I heard the *Nambour Variety Show*, I knew that this was a town that had to be visited. I learned that two famous Labor Party politicians had gone to Nambour High and gone on to rule the nation. Kevin Rudd and Wayne Swan were the Hawke and Keating of the 2000s, except they liked each other. At least a bit.

But this was just part of the incredibly rich musical townscape that I heard in this show. I loved it so much I asked the good people behind it, if I could recut it for the ABC and include it in the street series 'Greetings from…'. And that's sort of how I got to meet Hamish Sewell, the Svengali behind this amazing program about Nambour. With a $5,000-dollar community grant, he gathered a group of fellow ratbags and set about putting Nambour on the podcast map.

Hamish Sewell: We wanted to celebrate the town for all its history and for all its characters. Nambour is a very classy, bogan sort of place. When you live outside of a metropolitan city in a town like that you feel spoiled, because people are just so straightforward. That was where we started, and it had the history. It's one of the oldest kind of towns on the Sunshine Coast. It's the old sugar town, everyone still remembers the sugar mill. It was the main place from the 1930s through to about the 1970s. And it aspires to be, you know, probably on the coast, like Noosa or Maroochydore. But, it's what it is.

Words are perhaps not enough for Hamish to express his love for Nambour. But trust me, you have to listen to the show. It's the best of Australia, the worst and the most entertaining piece of audio I've heard in quite a while. What a soundtrack! Including *The Nambour Song*, which I had the pleasure of hearing many times in the edit suite. Then learning. It's three chords of magic.

THE NAMBOUR SONG
by Jamie Dunn

Empty shops in Currie Street
Sticky nights with searing heat
I sit and wonder where the cane train goes
Big pineapple macadamia nut
Sunday comes and everything's shut
Kentucky Fried but no Pizza Hut
All the sugar cane is filled with smut
I guess you could say we're living in a rut
Nambour as boring as bat shit
It's fucking awful but still I love it
Nambour not as bad as Townsville
Everyone bags it
But I never will

FRASER ISLAND: BUTCHULLA COUNTRY

The further north you go up Highway 1, the more tropo it feels. Keep going past wealthy but weird Noosa Heads, and we get to another old driving holiday destination from my youth that's pretty much ruined today. I guess I played a small part in it, but I'd prefer to blame dad. My father was an early adopter of the four wheel-drive phenomena, that's caused .08 of the rise in global temperatures.[44] In this first phase of the phenomena, the cars were often military-based vehicles. They were expensive and only available to well-paid professionals, such as doctors. Dad had a bright red jeep for a while and then a Land Rover. They were big and unwieldy and needed to be taken on holidays to roar around some pristine wilderness. Otherwise, what would be the point of them? I remember going on short trips with one specific aim – to get bogged. This was meant to be fun, and involved finding some mud or an impos-

---

44 A rough estimate off the top of my head. Also the blood alcohol level that used to be allowable in the ACT till it was lowered in 1991.

sible incline in the bush – then driving at full tilt into it. There would usually be another well-paid professional on hand with a winch on his four wheel-drive that would be used to extract our vehicle, and the fun would begin again. This could get tedious.

Fraser Island became a mecca for these early adopters, so off we went one year. It must have been around the mid-'seventies. Why don't we put 'The Bitch is Back' by Elton John on the 8-track cartridge. It seems appropriate to this highly destructive kind of road trip.

Fraser Island is a large sand island, the largest in the world I believe, with quite a history. The 1976 movie *Eliza Fraser* turned a confused story of shipwreck and Indigenous contact into a bawdy Aussie film. Suspense was maintained by the rags on Susanna York, the English actress who played the lead role. Would they ever come off? It was a silly film, but very popular in Australia and nowhere else. The film was one of the elements that

played a part in making Fraser Island a magnet for four wheeled drive enthusiasts. But the biggest attraction was the seemingly endless beach at low tide. Once you got your vehicle going on here, you were driving in an ad that conjured up lifestyle, freedom and possible fishing success.

At the stage we got our car onto the island, it was still a relatively unspoiled environment. You could drive for miles without seeing another car. Today, it's a racetrack for the superannuated, with a steady stream of 4x4s looping this magnificent place. Although the Indigenous name has been restored, it feels like something has gone wrong somewhere and it might be good to get these vehicles off K'gari. But I go back to my happy time there. I was a keen amateur photographer, as you have already learned. And on finding myself camping in ocean fronted wilderness, I wanted to take the leap into wildlife photography.

We had set up camp with a group of other families on some grassy sand hills just behind the ocean beach. Every night we had a campfire and it was here I heard rumours of the dingoes that roamed the island. Someone thought they had seen one in the distance, or maybe heard a howl. Apparently they were out there. I took it as my mission to prove it.

I had my trusty Konica C35 with me and wondered about luring one, close enough to get a photo. Apparently they came closer at night and there was suspicion of some canine rummaging in the food supplies. So my cunning plan involved a sausage on a piece of string. One night I tied the string to my toe and put the sausage at the other end, so that it was alluringly exposed outside my tent. I got in my sleeping bag with camera and flash nearby and waited.

Now the story gets pathetic. Silence descended on our campsite. Everyone went to sleep. But not me. There was no way I could sleep with the threat of being dragged out of bed by my toe by a savage dingo. Quietly, I slipped the string off and left the sausage where it was. The next morning it was gone, but I was still there. And it wasn't so long before a certain baby was taken by a dingo in the middle of Australia. But we'll come to that when we get to the Central Desert region.

Those camping holidays and the seduction of the sea, have stayed with me. Like many Australians I've been drawn to the watery perimeter that surrounds us. It's been a life. A lifestyle even.

GREY NOMADS

There's one group of drivers that have devoted their lives to lifestyle. For them the pinnacle of life itself could be the last phase. Where they drive off into the sunset and enjoy what this great country has to offer.

In my limited research for this book I have noticed a distinct polarisation in opinion when it comes to grey nomads. To some they are living the road dream we referred to early on, born somewhere on Route 66

in the 1950s. To others they are a whinging bunch of old white people clogging up the rural highways. I am old enough to be one and maybe I already am. So let's tread lightly – they are really just mature van lifers. Nostalgia for the road trip is a strong motivator for these people. I see them around the country. Huddled around fires at campgrounds, thermoses at the ready. They seem friendly enough. A little too friendly sometimes when you just want to slip past on the way to the shower block.

These people look like they have ample super to fuel their needs and have decided to see Australia while they still can. What's wrong with that? This seems a lot better than rotting in a retirement home or spending their days judging other people on Facebook. The great thing about being nomadic, is you can go anywhere! and so we will…

HOBART

MUWININA COUNTRY

DEVIL WORSHIP, COOKED CURD CHEESE AND FLANNELETTE

It's almost counter intuitive when older people retire to Tasmania. Shouldn't they be seeking warmer climes? Global warming may be changing this equation, but it's still very cold for quite a long time on this island in the middle of the Roaring Forties. And yet it's a spectacular place and somewhere I have spent a lot more time in recent years.

You don't often drive to Hobart from the 'mainland' any more. But you can still drive your vehicle to Port Phillip in Melbourne and onto a ferry that goes to Devonport in the north of Tasmania. Crossing Bass Strait can be unpleasant on occasions, due to the massive waves. Tom McCabe, the ex-VW mechanic who we heard from earlier, has taken up sailing in his mature years. He now works as a bosun (that's a real job) in Lindisfarne, a bay full of yachts in Hobart. He starts to look misty and serious when I ask him about crossing the straight.

> **Tom McCabe:** It's very shallow, only sixty metres. When there are strong currents and winds you can get these massive waves – and unlike out in the open ocean – they break.

So look at the weather before you book your car on the Spirit of Tasmania. That brings me to the band that I formed with Tom and another of our interviewees, Ivan Coates, from way back at the beginning (he waxed lyrical about American car culture and soft power). The Green Hats have only danced once and may never dance again. We gathered in Hobart for a band meeting and a photoshoot. We are a boy band full of old men that set a dinner party on fire with our choreographed ska moves, to Desmond Dekker's 'The Israelites'. The

---

MUSIC
- *The Israelites*, Desmond Dekker
- *Gone Daddy Gone*, the Violent Femmes

STAY
Airbnb has made life difficult for local renters. However, a really good one is Kylie's 'The Top Flat' in Mount Stewart. 'Stylish with great views'.

EAT
St Albi Bar and Eatery, Moonah, an excellent steakhouse on the fringe of the 'flannelette curtain'.

VISIT
Mona – Museum of Old and New Art – an obvious one. Not sure if I love everything in this heavy metal art collection, however you can drink the moment you get down to the basement. There's no doubt this place changed Hobart and the art gallery experience in general – for the better.

RANDOM POINT OF INTEREST
Check out the Tasman Bridge from a distance. If you look at the spacing of the pylons you'll see it's not even. The large space is where the bridge was hit by a ship – big news in 1975 – with scary looking photos of Holdens hanging off the edge. They never replaced the missing pylon!!

band is split down the middle about cars. Tom is a true enthusiast. If he somehow came into a large pool of money, he would 'buy a large house, hollow it out and fill it with a car collection. First car – a Ferrari 308'. Ivan, our more intellectual member, is 'more an A-to-B kind of guy'. I guess I'm in the agnostic zone, waiting for that electric vehicle that might mean something to me. Along with infrastructure, price and all that stuff. It's just these kinds of philosophical differences that can eat away at a band on tour. And then…

I was away from the guys a few days later. When…because of the odd nature of these difficult times, I was forced to isolate with my partner in the north of Tasmania in a lovely town not so very far from Southport. We'd lingered in NSW one day too many when a virus related decree came over the mobile phone from TAShealth. Stanley is about as isolated as you can get on an already isolated island. And so we continued isolating. It was there, while climbing up 'the Nut', a large unusual rock that Stanley is built around, that I started to think about the very nature of show business.

We began this tale speculating on the minstrels' journey, travelling the land from town to town, putting on shows for unsuspecting audiences. But the bigger the band, the less cost effective it is, and it gets harder to share the rider around. (that's all

the complimentary warm beer and cheese with crackers). Money often doesn't enter the equation. But what if you got rid of the people?

If the band was reduced to just the hats – it could really work well. We wouldn't have any creative differences, no solo projects, and no need for a rider. And of course it's already happening out there. We only have to look at competitions like the AI Eurovision. But the Green Hats go one step further – no music – just hats.

This detour to the north of Tasmania is really just to bring you my road trip recommendation. The Bass Highway (still route number 1, even here in Tassie) follows the coast from Launceston to the north-west corner. It's quite a road. Only in Tasmania do they put a double-laned carriageway on the beach so frequently. Often, you are driving beside the sea before turning into green hills, with mountains in the distance. Then there'll be a factory pumping out something on a beautiful headland. There's something not quite right about it, but it makes for an amazing drive. I'm almost thinking it's the top road I've been on in this country. That would make it five stars in the modern world!

And so we turn right after skirting the brooding town of Launceston, still on Highway 1 as we head down to Hobart. All the way passing some more high rating scenery. On to Hobart itself where the skinny old Tasman Bridge crosses the Derwent with the massive Mount Wellington/kunanyi hanging over it. A city with overwhelming scenery and a complicated history. What goes on here today?

Tom McCabe: We're pushing a boundary if we call Hobart a capital city, it's a large Australian town. And the draw card for me is really the sailing grounds as a yachtie. I just was completely seduced by the waterways around here. It's very laid back. I love the food and the fresh produce, the wine making, the craft beer. It's a much easier life compared to the hustle I was used to on the mainland. But I'm very glad I've made the move now in a sort of semi retirement role and working less and commuting far less and really enjoying it.

This sounded a bit too much like a superannuation ad. I had to go to his daughter for something a bit edgier.

Bernie McCabe: Downloading Tinder in Hobart is probably the worst thing you could do. Just because you'll probably know about 20 per cent of the people on there and the other 80 per cent probably know someone that you know. Everyone knows each other, but also doesn't hang out in the same groups. So there's a lot less like, void areas. It's not that you don't talk to anyone outside of your social circles. When I'm with my friends, and they seem to know every single person that we've walked down the street with, it's very strange. But they don't interact with them outside of that, which was one of the weird things when I moved here.

I happened to be there for the ultimate old person edgy experience. Dark Mofo. I wondered how this devil worship went down with the long term locals?

Tom McCabe: I don't know about the devil worshipping but I think there is some pagan roots behind the Charter of the festival, which really looks at the shortest day or the longest night of the year. I understand it was a challenge between the organiser David Walsh and his father, where David Walsh's father said, we could never get tourists into Hobart in the middle of winter. I think that may have been waving a red flag. But here we are. And we have great fun. It is a really nice celebration, and great to get out and party when it's otherwise damp, dark and dull.

What took me to Hobart most recently was another program in the 'Greetings from…' series for ABC Radio National. This time, I made a story about Elizabeth Street, the main road of Hobart. It's a great story about Art, the flannelette curtain (which everyone agreed starts at Creek Road on the edge of the suburb of Moonah), bikies, and gentrification gone wrong. It's the story of how this atmospheric city became an international star. In typical Hobart style, everyone I interviewed seemed to know everyone else I interviewed. It does have a large country town feel. As the urban architect Leigh Wooley told me: 'it's a small city in a large landscape'.

But don't let me bore you with more quotes from the program. Have a listen on good old Radio National, or more likely via the more modern but less fun medium that is the internet. It's called 'Greetings from Hobart' on RN *Earshot*.

LAUNCESTON: THERRERNOTEPANNER, LETERRERMAIRRENER AND PANNIHER COUNTRY

Elizabeth Street was always the main road north. And this road turns into Highway 1. While Hobart people might divided themselves into flannelette and non-flannelette people, there is an even bigger rivalry with the town at the end of this road. Launceston. According to my Hobart sources. Everything bad in the Tasmanian news comes from 'Launnie'. If there's a shooting – it's Launnie. If there's a break in – it's Launnie. But there's a good reason for this according to my Launceston source. Jill Cassidy, a long-term resident of this maligned town.

There's a problem there in that Launceston has the main court in Tasmania. The criminals get pulled into Launceston to be tried.

On questioning, it did appear that there was a 'good natured' rivalry between the two main cities of Tasmania. In Launceston, there is a perception that the people of Hobart live off the government, while Launcestrions generate income for the island.

The reasons being that the city is closer to the mainland and ships and planes can get there more easily. Also the fact that mining was mainly in the north and west.

The Tamar River in atmospheric Launceston.

This meant that Launceston could be considered the economic powerhouse of this magical island. But on further questioning, my source did back up some of my feelings about the city.

I've stayed there a number of times – always in winter – and there is a darker, more brooding atmosphere than even Hobart has. There seems to be a permanent fog hanging over the town and the turgid waters of the Tamar River often have an unhealthy looking froth floating by.

Nevertheless, it's a uniquely picturesque place, with steep hills, amazing looking old buildings and a kind of haunted feel. In fact, I confess to some extreme dreams of the supernatural variety, in one of the houses we stayed in. If ghosts do exist, they would definitely hang about Launceston.

Jill Cassidy: In the winter, there's a thermal inversion. Because of the way the hills are, and the way the river is, it means that all the cold and the smoke is trapped. And you can come over the hill from Hobart and there is this brown feeling all the way across the valley and it's revolting. They've actually done quite a lot to buyback wood heaters, for example. It's a difficult sort of climate. Summer is quite different.

This place is more 'Dark Mofo' than Hobart pretends to be! Long may the rivalry between the two Tasmanian cities continue and may the dark arts be the winner.

ARGENT STREET, BROKEN HILL

WILYAKALI COUNTRY

MUSIC
* *The Battle of Broken Hill,* Handsome Young Strangers
* *Wheels over the Desert,* the Lighthouse Keepers (why not?)

STAY
Palace Hotel, Argent Street, Broken Hill – it does have a party atmosphere at times, but why not!

EAT
Old McLeod's Bakery, 501–503 Chapple Street, Broken Hill.

THINGS OF INTEREST
Whites Mineral Art and Mining Museum – this is a fantastic little museum that 'Bushy' White has put together himself. He makes great art works out of minerals. Just the good side of *kitsch*. Sadly, the much loved Bushy has recently passed away, so it's unsure what will happen to this collection. Keep an eye out.

Bushy Whites mineral art works.

We're back on a road. A real road. The good old A32. The Barrier Highway. Where 140 km/h feels like 100 km/h. Goats to our left, goats to our right. We're going to the red centre, where the real Australia is supposed to exist. It's not only Americans who create myths from their interior. We do it too. The Australian version is just a bit more confused. America has mythologised every bolder and bullet riddled road sign, sending a steady stream of soft diplomacy out into the world. Toy cowboys sleep in children's bedrooms from Mumbai to Zanzibar. The Australian version is much less confident. There are a number of films that have been created in our 'dead heart'. There are also numerous band video clips where a bunch of guys get down amongst the dust and start ripping at their t-shirts. They don't need to plug their instruments into anything, it's already electric out here.

We are now driving through this cinematic landscape. It might be electrifying, but it's often flat and barren. Regardless, there's always something to surprise and engage the eye. We once spotted a nude cyclist out here on a hot day! Get ready to experience extreme variations in temperature depending on the season and time of day. But, the meditatory aspect of this journey, in the air conditioned comfort of a vehicle, is powerful. Perhaps a little too strong.

In the recent past, I was on the way to Broken Hill with my partner when we stopped at the mining town of Cobar, taking me back to a show the Lighthouse Keepers[45] had played there many years ago. In fact, due to a bushfire, it was two shows. The

---

[45] A plug for *Confessions of a Lighthouse Keeper,* if you want to read more on this.

band's meticulous records inform me that it was the sixteenth and seventeenth of January in 1985, at the New Occidental Hotel. The heat made the crowd extra edgy. The Lighthouse Keepers hit them with original songs like 'Wheels Over the Desert', which failed to gain any traction on the first night. In fact they groaned when we came on after they'd been dancing to the jukebox.

Juliet Ward, Lighthouse Keepers: We got stuck there for an extra night because there were bushfires. And so played a second night. And it was really weird because the same audience that despised us the night before, were actually singing along the second night. I think they just needed to know we were okay. It is one of my most pleasant memories.

It's a common Australian trait to be wary of strangers. It's probably an international one. Often, by simply hanging around for a while, people will begin to trust you and become hospitable. I thought about doing a tour and going back to some of those country towns and apologising for our self-indulgent sets. I'd be happy to play Jimmy Barnes for them, if that's what they want. Not sure about singing it. But would they remember an obscure 'eighties indie band that had caused slight irritation decades ago? I don't think so.

This time, the reason we were on the way to Broken Hill, was to record some interviews for an ABC Radio National series about streets called 'Greetings from…'. Just the names of the streets in Broken Hill were enough for me: Bromide Street, Oxide Street, Cobalt Street. I realised they were all minerals. The main street, Argent Street,

The Lighthouse Keepers play Cobar 1985 – hitting a six on the second night.

was a bit fancier, using the French word for silver. It's wide and full of imposing looking buildings that date back from the eighteenth century mining boom that town is built upon. It's literally built upon it, as the mine runs underneath these streets and a huge slag heap (or mullock heap if you want to use the fancy local term) dominates the skyline. Every morning and every evening at a quarter-to-seven you can feel the mine beneath, as they detonate charges.

Blake Griffiths, Broken Hill Art Gallery:
It's kind of the same feeling as if someone is stealing your wheelie bin. You can hear it happening, it feels a bit distant. But you definitely know that something is unsettling.

But Broken Hill, which gave the multinational company Broken Hill Proprietary Company Ltd (BHP) its name, is not just about mining. It's a town that's attracted creative types from way back. As well as fine artists, Broken Hill has a history of films that date back to *Wake in Fright* in 1971, a film directed by the Canadian–Bulgarian Ted Kotchef. It has become a cult classic for good reason. It's a strange film, full of aggressive hard drinking characters, kangaroo violence and heat stroked scenes. It set the tone for all the films that followed. *Mad Max* and *Priscilla Queen of the Desert* both owe something to the spirit of this film. I think Australian art works best when it goes a bit left of centre and explores the weird mix of characters that make this country. Having a Canadian–Bulgarian direct a film written by a Jamaican poet from a book by an Australian documentary maker, acted by a mix of English and Australian actors, not to mention unwilling wildlife, is a perfect example. It doesn't always work. I've dabbled in the art form myself, with mixed results. But when it does work – it feels like something worthwhile. I think Australian cinema got very lost in attempting to be high art, sometime in the 'nineties. So far it's struggled to get back from there, with occasional exceptions. And if I'd actually seen any recent Australian films I'd be able to comment more meaningfully.

It was in Broken Hill that I met a man who had lived 'Wake in Fright'. The central character is an outsider who struggles with alcohol in an outback town as things get weird. Broken Hill is the perfect setting for an alcoholic rock writer to dry out. I seemed to have ended up knowing quite a few rock journalists from the heyday of this literary genre. In Australia in the 'seventies and 'eighties, we had magazines like *RAM* and *Juke*, augmenting our imported *NME* and *Rolling Stone* magazines.[46] These papers were thick with black ink that would come off in your sweaty hands, as you imbibed the gospel according to whoever was giving it to you straight. These guys (many of them were male) are themselves characters, often prickly, often opinionated, but I like them that way. Especially once they've lost the power to review you, which always makes the relationship a bit stressful.

Jack Marx: I tried to be a rock star and didn't make it. And people seized upon that. 'You're writing because you're jealous and you hate all rock stars.' But I don't think so. I think, if anything, I sort of knew what was driving those guys.

---

46 Yes, there was an Australian *Rolling Stone* magazine.

In Broken Hill, I met Jack Marx in person for the first time, even though we'd been in the same venues at the same time back in the Sydney indie rock 'eighties. He'd been a writer at the tail end of rock journalism's heyday. In this period, street press such as *On The Street* started to come out for free. It became harder for these scribes to make a living. This could force them into unusual circumstances. Like working for movie stars. In the new century, Jack found himself being courted by Australian and New Zealand's very own bad boy, Russell Crowe. A movie star who really wanted to be a Rock Star. Dreams that were not unlike Jack's own.

Jack Marx: He wanted to be a musician but he became a successful actor, and some part of him thought 'the musician in me needs to have a voice'. But he can't write songs. Like a lot of people can't write. A lot of people learn to play the guitar. And then think they can write songs. And Russell's one of those. A really telling moment. I was talking to Russell one night about the concept of the 'unfuckable' song, the song that can't be destroyed, no matter how bad you are. And my idea for that song was 'The First Time Ever I Saw Your Face' You know, various people have done that song and they've all done fantastic versions. Joe Dolce would have done a good one. And Russell's vote for the unfuckable song was 'Molly Malone'. That's not a song.

It all sounded very believable to me, as I'd heard other Russell Crowe stories from people who had met and worked with him. And of course there was the 'Go Russ Go!' story. Which is pure fact and needs no citation or explanation. Maybe we do have something America wants. Tough guys. Even though Russell is a mix of New Zealandish and Australian, let's accept that accolade gracefully. There's a few other examples of Aussie tough guys that need to be imported into a land that you think would be full of them. Russell definitely out-toughs Tom Cruise for example.

Anyway, Russ basically wanted Jack to write a good review of him. Starting with his music. A publicist in other words. Jack refused Russell's money, but accepted all the expenses he could drink. He ended up writing one article about the movie, *Cinderella Man*. But it wasn't sycophantic enough for Russell. So he was off the job. "Perhaps you should stop jerking off and just write books," was how Russell ended the last email.

Then Jack decided to come clean about the process online, in 2005, in a piece called 'I Was Russell Crowe's Stooge'.[47] The resulting story wasn't what Russell wanted at all. This story about writing for the great man took the reader on a mind trip through what it takes to be a publicist for a middle-aged brat. It's what happens when the wrong sort of character is waited on hand and foot and gets everything they desire and more. Russell let it be known that Jack could have a good life, island holidays, whatever he wanted. Did Jack break some journalistic code of ethics by refusing this life and revealing the emperor's new clothes? Public relations is really at the core of what remains of journalism and Jack didn't play the game.

However, this story was a breakthrough for Jack as a journalist. It ended up in print in the Fairfax papers after going viral online. A new phenomenon at the time, Jack even won a Walkley Award for it. But he never heard from Russell Crowe again. Well, it was a kind of a breakthrough. He hasn't written a lot of paid articles since. In fact, it was part of the journey that sent Jack to Broken Hill, a broken man, drinking heavily. By then, his marriage had collapsed and he found himself living the life of a fictional character in his favourite Australian film *Wake in Fright*!

Jack Marx: It's a film about the extremes of the Australian character. For me, it's also a metaphor of the horrors. The horrors such a serious drinker goes through when they stop drinking. Something that began afflicting me, only when I came to Broken Hill. John Grant, the main character in *Wake in Fright*, that's very much his problem. If he just keeps drinking like everyone else. He'll be fine.

Jack Marx drove to Broken Hill in 2012. He's still living there. I've now met him there a few times, and even put on a live show with him and the ABC Radio National team at the Palace Hotel. He came on stage in his adopted outfit of Akubra hat and moleskin jacket and delivered a ripper trivia Kahoot.[48] The crowd went slightly wild. It transpired Jack had become a somewhat divisive figure in Broken Hill and had lost his job at the local ABC for reading the news a bit too drunkenly. But, of course, that only adds to the Marx myth.

Jack Marx: That's a very common story in Broken Hill, an awful lot of the people who weren't born here, never intended to come here on purpose. Rick Ball, an artist in town, was on his way to Europe, and had some time to kill before his flight left, and never made it. He's still here. A lot of stories like that. I think it's something about the isolation

---

47 www.smh.com.au/national/i-was-russell-crowes-stooge-20060607-gdnp6a.html

48 Kahoot is an online quiz program. Many people will know it.

Ando's artwork is 'the world's largest acrylic painting on canvas by a single artist' – 12 x 100 metres.

that does it. For me going through a divorce, it was horrible. But, whenever I was coming back from the coast, after going back to see my kids, I could almost feel the stress leaking out onto the road. And that's road therapy at its most powerful.

It's not only drunken writers. Broken Hill attracts artistic types like iron to a magnet. They are drawn by the landscape, the cheap accommodation and by other artists. Pro Hart is perhaps the best known of the original art pioneers, 'the brushmen of the bush', but many have come and many remain here. Pro Hart might be slightly embarrassing to true art aficionados but he is well remembered in the local community. He mentored a young Indigenous carver, Badger Bates, who's now mentoring a new generation of carvers. I met Badger over several trips. I even did a bit of carving with him. It was very therapeutic. According to him, he's in such demand by the media, that lapel microphones grow off him. He also told us just a little of his incredible history. He grew up on the banks of the nearby Barka River, or the Darling as it was called by Europeans. He's spent a lot of energy fighting for Indigenous water rights for this river. It's a wonder to see it, even now it's a remnant of what it used to be when it was wide and clear. A big river flowing out here in the hot arid middle of Australia.

Badger Bates: I lived across the river in a tin hut and never went to school. We didn't have much money. But the old people, they'd sit me down and I'd learn how to carve boomerangs and stuff like that. And then from that I got a job in national parks because old granny and mum showed me things about the bush. Broken Hill is a funny place. I think it draws a lot of people because there's a lot of artists around. When I went to Broken Hill I was scared of doing art work. You don't have to be a black person to get scared in the art world. Other people were there, people like Pro Hart. Because I used to carve things on emu eggs but never tried lino before.

Everyone seemed to know everyone in Broken Hill. One of Badger's artistic circle, Asma d. Mather is another artist who moved from Melbourne and has become involved in the local arts scene. She's a practicing Sufi, a Muslim sect, that tends towards the mystical. She rents a huge house in the middle of town, with a freedom to make art that the economics of Melbourne do not allow. There were also other factors in the big cities that made Broken Hill attractive at the time I went there.

Asma d. Mather: We can see from the COVID situation, just the beginning of what it's like to be in a city when something happens, like you've got a high concentration of people. I think part of what is happening to our knowledge systems is that our concentration is being fragmented. I mean, I'm not an expert on this, I'm really an artist. There's a history here of Sufism. The Afghans came in the late-1800s to deliver water and supplies to all the inland regions. The oldest surviving mosque is in Broken Hill.

The history of Broken Hill obviously goes a long way back before they started digging for silver. The original Hill was shaped like an anchor and stood out from the surrounding landscape. It is now completely covered by a slag heap. The slag heap itself has been heritage listed.

Badger Bates: When Broken Hill wasn't settled, it came from the bronze wing pigeon story. Back in the Dreaming, a fella tried to get a flock of bronze wing pigeons with a net, one escaped and they threw boomerangs and all that, and it flew towards Broken Hill. And because it was wounded. When it was going around, if you look at the colour, the feathers, the bronze wing pigeons got pretty colours in it. It's the minerals in the ground. And that's like the old people tell us.

Asma d. Mather: I find it very interesting that the guardians of this country, the Aboriginal people, say to put the earth back how you find it by the end of the day. The Sufi say, don't move a rock without replacing it.

There were such a range of characters I got to meet in Broken Hill. It was a reflection of where Australia is at today. Darriea Turley, Broken Hill's first female mayor,

has part Afghan heritage and a husband who works beneath her in the enormous mines. 'Bushy' Whyte, a retired miner who had devoted his later life to making art out of the minerals he had dug up, produces fantastic works that stay just this side of *kitsch*. Mick Schinella, a third-generation European shop owner with a raspy laugh, went underground as a kid and never went back there.

Then there's the Palace Hotel. Esther La Rovere, a theatrically-inclined Australian with Italian heritage, is now managing director and co-owner of this famous watering hole.

Esther La Rovere: If the walls could talk, I think there would be a lot of laughter.

Esther's own history is intertwined with the hotels'. Her parents were part of the Italian

The Palace Hotel.

diaspora drawn to Broken Hill by mining. Esther left the town in her youth to seek her fortune on the European festival circuit in the mid-2000s. She toured with a band called 'the Hauntingly Beautiful Mousemoon' that morphed into a fringe cabaret show. On her way home she stopped off in India for six months. As you did.

Esther: My sister rang me from Australia out of the blue and said, The Palace is up for sale. We're thinking of putting up a bid.

Esther was born in Broken Hill in the 1970s, making her an 'A grader'. The A-B-C grading system is unique to the city and goes back to the early mining days. It has continued as an informal class signifier. 'B graders' were people who were new to town, but had married an 'A grader'. 'C graders' were everyone else who blew into town. They were considered less reliable underground. If you were an 'A Grader', you had a job whenever you wanted it – no worries. So an A grader with a theatrical touch! Who better to run the iconic Palace Hotel.

Esther: It's like a big moored cruise liner stuck in the desert. There's over 500 square metres of murals painted all around this building. Renaissance meets the outback.

These aren't ordinary murals. They are an eclectic range of landscapes, waterscapes and fake European masters evoking an outback Bavarian schnitzel house. The hotel is also full of stuffed animals and exotic statues. An enterprising Italian migrant called Mario Celotto was responsible for the hotel's change in décor. He purchased the Palace when it was at a low ebb in the mid-1970s. The town's population was beginning to decline as the mines were mechanised.

Esther: Mario was a family friend, a very colourful fellow. He bought the Palace

The Palace Hotel, a mineral artwork by 'Bushy' Whyte.

a chicken in reception. That scene made it to the final film. The Palace was the perfect film set for the whacky movie that Stephan had imagined. No set dressing required.

But all this accidental history came late to the Palace. It was originally built as a coffee house, funded by a temperance movement group, in the hope of providing a palace of sober culture in one of the biggest drinking towns in the nation. It had a ladies lounge and a men's smoking room. But it was not a success. A few years later

when it was getting a bit dilapidated, and it became Mario's Palace.

The murals are largely the work of an Indigenous artist, Gordon Waye. Mario commissioned them after he'd had a go at painting a version of Botticelli's *Venus* on the foyer ceiling. He decided it was too much like hard work. Mario's main instruction was to include water, to make the hotel feel like an 'oasis in the desert.'

But, it was an unlikely hit film that really turned the Palace's fortunes around. The 1994, drag queen road movie, *Priscilla Queen of the Desert*, featured a number of scenes in the hotel. The Palace almost wasn't in the film, because the council's location guide didn't think it was worth showing to prospective film productions.

Esther: There was probably a bit of an embarrassment about the hotel. It certainly wasn't cool to be *kitsch* or retro, in the early 'nineties. People liked glitz and glamour. Luckily, the hotel missed all of those renovations of the 'eighties and 'nineties.'

The location guide's reticence piqued the interest of the film's director, Stephan Elliot, who went to look for himself. The first thing he came across was Mario stuffing

it became just another pub, albeit a classy one. For a while there were seventy-five working pubs in Broken Hill. This was a town full of rich thirsty miners.

Esther: When Broken Hill first began the workers were becoming the elite, because they were making so much money. They were just boundary riders or people who happened to be in the right place at the right time. Part of the fervour of the mining game was that anyone could come out here and make their fortune.'

The miners were paid well, but they also lived hard, dangerous lives. They loved a drink, and didn't respond well to any laws that restricted their intake – like six o'clock closing in the 1960s. So the Palace Hotel beckoned to them, even underground. Esther sometimes takes visitors below the pub into the cellar to show them just how close the mines are. A closed shaft can be seen where miners used to enter the Palace from below.

Esther: As the miners were digging some of these really long shafts that go under different parts of the city, they decided to dig themselves an entry to the downstairs bar at the hotel.

Miners could clock on for work below, make their way up to the Palace Hotel and start drinking early, then go back down and clock off.

By the time Esther clocked on as the Palace Hotel's manager, in the 2000s, her experience on the European festival circuit, combined with the *Priscilla* movie, gave her an idea. An annual drag festival 'The Broken Heel', centred at the Palace Hotel now takes place every September – virus willing.

> **Esther:** The festival has been going for six years, for our first three years, our biggest ticket audience were females over the age of fifty-five. It just seemed to be like a big gaggle of women out with their girlfriends ready to have a hoot of a weekend. Just so much laughter!

Maybe that laughter echoes the past. Grey nomads and millennials on druggy road trips now join the ancient cackles of miners sneaking a few quick ones while on duty. Could the Palace's revival be a sign that Broken Hill is back in business?

It was in this hotel in 2020 that I met up with Justine Clarke, the Australian actor and musician, who I'd recently been working with. But this time we had masks at the ready. It was peak coronavirus, even though it had barely touched Broken Hill. Justine's mask looked pretty handy for avoiding fans actually. I'd seen it first hand when we filmed a TV series.

Every child and parent from a certain *Playschool* era would make a beeline for her and get a selfie. She dealt with it very politely. On this occasion, she was in Broken Hill filming a reversion of *The Flying Doctors* for Channel 7. I learned what a 'procedural' meant. It's one of those long serial TV dramas where there is a body and a convoluted sequence of clues and odd people that revolve around nice scenery.

In other words, a screen version of the rural crime story we learned about earlier in this journey. Perfect for Broken Hill. Justine feels part of the film-making tradition that has gravitated here.

I did play in Broken Hill with the Lighthouse Keepers when younger. Tiny crowd but big pay due to the Musicians Union. Looks like free beer too!

> **Justine Clarke:** I do feel part of that tradition, one because there are so many projects filmed here, but also because the Mad Max II museum is in Silverton just down the road and I was in *Mad Max III*, so it was pretty great going out there. It feels a bit like family.

And the pub next to the Mad Max II museum is the Silverton Hotel. This is probably the real metaphysical core of the nuggety Australia that all those films try to bring to life. The Palace Hotel had a flamboyant mural makeover in the 'seventies, but this place has stayed fixed in a mythical time. A place where a gnarled outback character might grab a beer or ten. The bar inside has been seen in countless sequences in films and ads, it feels like home. It's become a bit of a tourist trap but you can also get a refreshing ale there. You can also get a beer in many places around Broken Hill. It's a town devoted to drinking.

Be careful you don't wind up in Broken Hill at a bar for the next decade, having one more drink for the road. Let's keep on trucking. Indeed trucks are a big feature of the drive now. Watch out for them. I find I can drive a lot faster out here, and it's unpredictable trucks and kangaroos that are the biggest danger. Still, it's amazing how much more confidently you can drive when you can see so far ahead on a good road.

Sections of this chapter can be heard on the *Earshot* documentary, 'Greetings from Broken Hill', ABC Radio National – abc.net.au/rn

AUSTRALIA ACROSS

WHEELS ACROSS THE DESERT

MUSIC
* *The Seabirds*, the Triffids
* *Walking on a Dream*, Empire of the Sun
* *The General Calling*, the Panics

EAT
Papa Luigis Café – Fremantle

STAY
Travis Jay Myles had a great time escaping his fourth floor room in a quarantine hotel using the old rope made from sheets method. Try the Great Eastern Motor Lodge, Rivervale, Perth.

RANDOM POINT OF INTEREST
Perth is closer to Bali than Canberra.

The long section of Highway 1 that runs from Adelaide to Perth is a drive that gives you an idea of just how big this country is. The Eyre Highway is very long, very straight and usually very hot. We are now driving across the great Australian Bight, on the very lip of it. If you get out of your car for a moment and wander 100 metres to the side, you'll be horrified by the alarmingly high cliffs you are so close to. I imagine this has been a nasty end for at least a few drunken travellers. The Australian continent is weirdly tilted to the North. The cliffs of the Bight are the high part at the south end. Way up north in the gulf, the land is low and tends towards crocodile infested mangroves. Here on the windy cliffs that plunge into deep ocean, we sense the great white sharks that travel a parallel route. As you make this endless drive you have plenty of time to think about the dark shapes below. The Triffids' 'The Seabirds' plays as you try to navigate your own internal beasts. The Nullarbor plain is tedious, disturbing and magnificent.

But wait! At the time of writing there's a formidable barrier to our journey. There's a whole new area of homeland security that's booming. In 2019, I was pretty irritated when I was taken into an interview booth, questioned and fined for having a few bananas in the car as we crossed between Victoria and South Australia. Gone were the days when they took it from you and politely put it in a bin. But 2020 made that seem like a quaint bureaucratic procedure. The borders have become real and there's a philosophical Trumpian Wall between Western Australia and the rest of the country. The recent virus drama has highlighted the fact that Western Australia doesn't seem to want to be part of our great nation anymore. Who knows what will happen by the time you read this?

Eddy Jokovich, New Politics: There was actually a secessionist vote in 1933: Western Australia voted to secede from the rest of Australia, but the King said, 'no, you can't do that'. So that's it, for eighty-eight years the state has been wanting to leave the rest of the Federation. But it's sort of still here. And I think, psychologically, it's done quite a lot of damage to Western Australia being in this relationship it doesn't want to be in. It's damaging for the rest of the states as well.

It seems Western Australia is not alone in the secessionist feelings anymore. Queensland has mixed feelings as do many of the other states. But let's move forwards, not backwards. I met Rob McComb from the Triffids way back in the 'eighties when we played music together and it was with pleasure, myself and Eddy Jokovich spoke across three states to record a podcast. One locked down in Victoria, and one in hotel quarantine in Western Australia and the other roaming free in NSW. As happens with a grisled bunch of ex-musos, we talked about the old days in Perth.

Rob McComb, the Triffids: Perth is so much more changing in its physical landscape than somewhere like Melbourne in terms of venues. In Melbourne, Bruce Milne and Mary Mihelakos run a little musical history tour around the venues. There's that much intact. Last time I was in Perth I was driving around trying to find venues that we used to play and they are mostly not there or completely renovated. In Australia, we don't protect our cultural heritage very well. And Western Australia is probably up there with the best in the negligence stakes.

Not in Perth, but close enough – Europe 1985 with the Triffids. The word 'selfie' has been attributed to an Australian David Hope in 2002. So these cranky people didn't understand the selfie thing yet – but I'm there in front – at the cutting edge. Me, Rob McComb and Lee Vergona on the way to a show in Rotterdam.

1985: The Lighthouse Keepers are so excited to get to the Indian they perform a ritual with a bottle of water from the Pacific.

The only venue from that era Rob could find was Mojos in Fremantle. It used to go by the name of the Stoned Crow, and both me and Rob had played there in the 'eighties and most likely got stoned, possibly at the same time. But do we really need to preserve these cultural sites? They were often unattractive buildings that were really just enclosures for what went on inside. They have a Go-Betweens Bridge in Brisbane. It seems the antithesis of what this band were doing. A Triffids Motel, maybe, somewhere down south near Mandurah.

Perth is bright, harsh, and a world away from the east. It was logical for the Triffids to go to London, it seemed just as close as the east coast. Although they made the Nullarbor road trip many times. There's a lot of recent British migrants amongst the mix in Perth, and perhaps that's why they got their *New Musical Express* magazines a little earlier in the days of punk.

Eddy Jokovich, New Politics: I got introduced to punk music and new wave and everything – because I lived near the Perth Airport and the delivery of the *NME* used to come in every Friday night, at about nine o'clock. I'd ride my bike to the Airport. Then, reading the *NME*, I thought, well, if Sid Vicious can play the guitar, so can I.

In the 'eighties, Perth threw up a diverse bunch of acts like the Triffids, the Stems, the Scientists and (sort of) the Hoodoo Gurus. When I played there I remember lots of indie type bands like Rabbits Wedding, novelty acts like the Jam Tarts and a vast suburban network of cover bands. It has continued impressively over the years. The Panics, Sleepy Jackson, Tame Impala, (sort of) Empire of the Sun and a long list that will aid your journey considerably. What was it about this hot blustery city on the edge of the continent at the end of the world that begats musical seekers? It's definitely worth a visit and I'll be back there if I'm ever allowed. For the moment we remember the days when the Eyre Highway wasn't a road to nowhere.

Blak Douglas, artist/musician: The Eyre Highway is something to experience in itself for those who haven't done it. The Elders in my life told me how they used to drive that one. Of course it wasn't sealed back then. So if you had rain, then the semis would just perforate the road. It didn't matter what car you were in. If it wasn't up to standard, then you're going to be on the side fixing a driveshaft or an axle. And I hear of all these stories and think: 'the poor buggers'. Now it's sealed the whole way.

Brad Owen, Bathurst Museum: If you drive your car across the Nullarbor Plain, you'll hear all the funny noises, whether it's going to mean that the car makes it or not, you'll hear all that stuff.

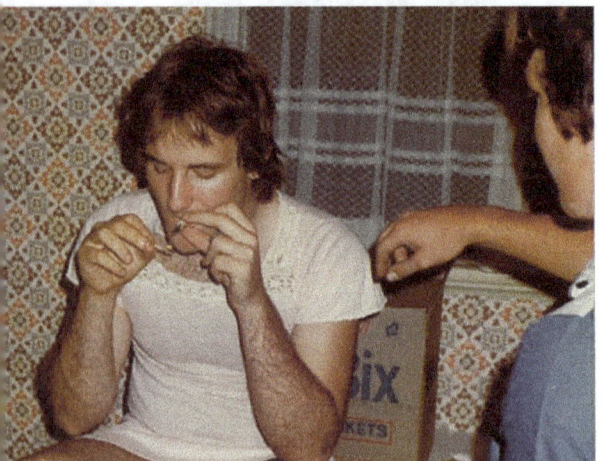

Driving back from Perth to Adelaide is too much. Once is enough.

As we head towards our next destination, I wonder if I have accidentally created a procedural myself. In book form.

A nuggety bloke was last seen buying a slab of Emu Bitter[49] at Eucla. His EH Holden wagon is found on the side of the road near the edge of the Great Australian Bight. The copyrighted flute section from Down Under plays as the drone takes us up. We drift through this amazingly filmic landscape. So vast and bright that no lens can capture it properly. We must use our imagination. The death of Australia. The possible suspects? Globalism, Trump, the internet mob, grey nomads, the new left, the new right, it could be anyone or anything. Are we a country anymore? I don't think we can blame the virus, it's actually been responsible for some moments of togetherness. We've already passed a few. But let's just enjoy the mesmerising scenery as we head north!

---

49 The classic Perth beer, Emu piss (a.k.a. Bush Chooks, according to Neil Pfister), is now made in South Australia!

ALICE SPRINGS: THE CROSSROADS

ARRERNTE COUNTRY

MUSIC
* Beethoven: *Moonlight Sonata*, Presto Agito
* *Jailanguru Pakarnu*, Warumpi Band (from Papunya)

STAY
DoubleTree Hilton Hotel, Alice Springs. I know I shouldn't, but I really liked this place.

EAT
DoubleTree Hilton Hotel, why not eat there too, it's pretty good.

THINGS OF INTEREST
Pine Gap, the infamous American base, is very close. It's part of the weird mix that makes up this crossroads town. All the gaps are interesting. Yeperenye/Emily Gap, is close to town and can feel quite unsettling at certain times of the day. It's like a doorway to another dimension. There's more gaps across the magnificent MacDonnell Ranges.

Blak Douglas, artist: The cloud formations are consistently these flat bottom clouds. And then your arid landscapes, all of these would come together to create my generic template landscape, Then I put something in the foreground that is generally of a political nature.

Frances Green: There's a transient sort of nature to a lot of those towns where people are moving through, or they're ending up there to run away or whatever. So there is that kind of edge to a place like Alice. There was one memory I have of stopping at a service station, on the way to Alice. And in the freezers, there were these frozen kangaroo tails. They were used as a weapon to hold up the station. I think in the territory or in those remote locations, you do see scenarios that are a bit surreal.

Alice Springs is sort of near Uluru. Only 500 kilometres away. Close in outback terms. It was built around a telegraph station in the days when getting a wire all the way from the UK to Australia was a big thing. Broken Hill might symbolise the dead heart in an INXS video clip, but Alice Springs feels like the real middle. I was blown away when I got there the first time. This was well into the twenty-first century. I was mainly surprised by the landscape. I had imagined this central desert area to be more of the classic flat Australian desert landscape, with maybe a bit of scrub. Something like Mulga country. But it was neither flat nor desert. The landscape is all over the place, and there's an amazing variety, just around Alice Springs itself. Taking a loop around Namatjira Drive is quite something. Craggy mountains, weird rock formations, every corner turned brings a new vista.

We're now on the ultimate guts of Australia road – the A87 – the Stuart Highway. Straight through the middle. It's a shortcut across Highway 1. As we go even further into the outback, and the red dust gets into everything we carry, I wouldn't mind hearing the 'Presto Agitato' section of Beethoven's *Moonlight Sonata*. There's some great music in the classics, though there is a lot that's hard going for the uninvested listener. So let's play one of the very best pieces as we meditate on the vista through the windscreen.

Then water! I was very surprised to find rivers and swimming holes. It flooded one day. And the Todd River flowed in front of us.

The heat was more expected. But the lifestyle in these parts is based around minimum movement when hot. Air conditioning has smoothed out any rough edges that would have made life in the telegraph station days pretty hard. Of course, the Arrernte people have been there long before telephones. Alice Springs today has a very eclectic mix of Indigenous people from all around the central desert, earnest European types, hard core Akubra Aussies, tourists on their way to Uluru, and everything in between, giving it a slightly mad feel. It's quite intoxicating. Sometimes literally, as alcohol is big in the Northern Territory. It is a big issue as well, that I won't attempt to get into. For me, it was a place where you can feel the long Indigenous history very close. Just around Alice is a ring of rugged hills, with gaps that feel like portals into other dimensions.

John Ogden is a writer, photographer and filmmaker who ended up spending a lot of time in Central Australia.

John Ogden: I was in London '75 and got accused of being privy to the genocide of Australian Aborigine and it stung. I felt really dumb. I didn't know anything about the First People in my own country. It wasn't something you were taught in school in the 'fifties and 'sixties. That great Australian silence. So I came back. I started studying anthropology and did a couple of units. One was traditional Aboriginal culture, how their culture and societies worked. The second one was on legislation since colonisation, post contact legislation, that really threw me because I just didn't realise the extent of the bastardries that happened to Australian aborigines. People who want to learn about Aboriginal culture – that's where you go. The central deserts... the western desert. Because it's really powerful. I if I talk about the deep spirituality of Aboriginal beliefs now — a lot of people would think I'm a fruitcake and I don't really want to go into it here — but there were some people I know, scientists who went out there and started talking about all sorts of things, that would be considered paranormal by today's standards. And this is scientists talking.

Another small town not far away from Alice in central desert distances is Papunya. Just 350 kilometres west on a red dirt road. It's well known today as the centre for Papunya Tula art movement. Papunya has had a difficult history and the backstory to this art movement is quite incredible. Papunya was always a desert crossroads. But white assimilation policy of the 1960s created a settlement of government buildings and looped roads. Here groups of desert people were forced together, mainly the Pintupi, Luritja, Walpiri, Arrernte, and Anmatyerre. It was an uncomfortable mix, and the dodgy housing and imperious European overlords made it extra unpleasant.

Geoffrey Bardon, Papunya Special School art teacher, 1971: (from Papunya, a place made after the story) The great native camps surrounding the whitefella town circumscribed it and hemmed it in, with its lawns and flower gardens, its planted trees and white painted stones...many of these white people of my experience were seemingly a detritus of our culture, yet they held great power over the lives and destinies of the Aboriginal people at Papunya settlement

We began this journey staring at some ants on a driveway in Canberra in the 'seventies. It seems like a long time ago. Coincidentally it was around the same time a renegade art teacher was approached by a group of Pintupi elders. They had seen him encouraging children to turn traditional sand drawings into paintings. In 1971, *Honey Ant Dreaming* mural was painted on the Papunya school wall. It was an artwork with many complex layers and meanings and the starting point for an Australian Aboriginal art renaissance that swept the whole world. It was painted over by a maintenance worker in 1974. The Sydney artist Blak Douglas travelled there in 2001 to learn from some of the senior artists of this movement.

Blak Douglas, artist: It was just an amazing whirlwind dream journey, I got to sit down with some of the last remaining male painters and the originators of the Papunya Tula movement. I got to learn the reason for the styles and the stories. And coming back with that fuel, to the eastern seaboard. It's an easy thing to sell. And that's what you'll see at the forefront of most tourist shops. All the other Koori artists around me were painting dots. I was constantly puzzled why people still just stuck at painting a style, which is obviously poached from that mob. So I vehemently steered away from it and focused on producing my own style. And that was based on that road trip to Papunya where you have those red dirt roads. And so my clouds

Man On The Goon by Blak Douglas.

are white and puffy, like government, and they float in for a period. And then they float away. And then you've got the roads that consistently reach a vanishing point, that's a metaphor for an uncertain future or uncertain past. So many people are finding their identity. And some people never find it. In those remote regions old people will pass, and young kids aren't taking it on. The road is a metaphor.

The top end is definitely a world unto itself. It's like another country compared with the southern cities. They remain a territory, with ultimate legislative powers remaining in the commonwealth. Like Australia hanging on to the Queen as head of state, it's just a bit too hard to make the population care. They were part of South Australia from 1863 to 1911, which stretches the idea of what South means. The telegraph line that made Alice Springs what it is, was key to the massive state. But the Northern Territory of South Australia was a financial burden and they divorced. It's all part of the weird history of this land of deadly creatures.

No wonder that it didn't seem out of place to the rest of the nation, when a baby went missing there in 1980. Uluru was Ayers Rock at the time, and the newspaper headlines never stopped. At this point in history the mainstream press were all powerful and

Chris Tangey tells some TV people the real story.

could push a story in any direction they wanted. Selling papers and tapping into the reptilian part of the reader's brain was what it was all about. Does that sound so very different from today? For some real fake news, you just have to go back to the 'eighties when a national mystery involving a dingo, a baby and some Christians of a lesser known sect held the nation captive. Meryl Streep has turned Lindy Chamberlain's words into a catch phrase, but at the time the news stories about Lindy's child Azaria, going missing at Ayers Rock were everywhere.

The stories were on all media available at the time: TV, radio, magazines and newspapers, but personally I remember phasing out at a certain point. It was just too much, something had hit a nerve with the Australian public that I didn't quite get. The mythic dead-heart-of-Australia story had come to life with a strange cast. Dingo, baby, odd religious people and the heat hazed backdrop of a huge rock in the middle of the country. It was the tale Australia wanted to hear.

Many years later, I was working on a documentary with an Alice Springs drone pilot called Chris Tangey. He had lived in Alice for thirty years and fitted in seamlessly with the extremely eclectic group of permanent residents in town. We got talking one night, and sure enough Chris knew the real story behind Azaria Chamberlain's disappearance. For those who don't know, Lindy was convicted of Azaria's murder and sent to jail in 1981; she was released in 1986, eventually compensated in 1992 and further exonerated in 2012. But Chris had the inside on the dingo itself. I switched on my handy recording device. Here's the story with all names except the dingo's removed. Just in case.

Chris Tangey: I heard that there was a dingo that used to hang around the campground, his name was Ding. And not far away was a ranger's house. And one of the rangers who lived there, was the son of a top Northern Territory official. I refer to them as territory royalty. In those days, it was even a smaller place than it is now. Even though it's two and a half times the size of Texas, there were less than 200,000 people back then. Anyway, the story was that he used to surreptitiously feed this dingo called Ding, who used to come up to his house. He knew he was doing the wrong thing, but you know, harmless. The story was that Ding was the one that took the baby that night. And there were two trackers who actually tracked the dingo back towards his house and were taking the police back with them. They were saying things like, 'we can see he's carrying something here. He rested down here', as they went along the tracks. And the police are going 'No, no can't be that way. That's the ranger's house, it can't go that way now.' Yes. Now look, he's going this way. He's going this way. He's going this way. And the police, as I was told, called it off and said you're going totally the wrong way. And because the trackers had actually been drinking that night, their evidence was given as inadmissible. So it never entered the fray of the entire run of investigations. And there were many. So as I understand it, the ranger rang his dad in a panic. His dad contacted the Chief Minister and it sort of went out from there. This can't go any further. So there's two things here. One was the royalty side of it. The other is that, here is one of their own Northern Territory government employees, causing the death of a tourist in their most important industry, just stupidity. And at that time, the rock was incredibly important to tourism and still is today. I mean, there's no bigger product than Uluru.

Mystery solved. The Territory is full of stories and storytellers. It may all be true. Crocodile Dundee is supposedly based on a true character but what does that really mean? There's a lot of croc talked up there, it makes life interesting.

The thing about the Northern Territory is that there are plenty of real crocodiles there. I had an unpleasant experience with some near Darwin when I was making youth TV in the 'nineties. Some young guys took me out in a tinnie 'croc hunting', which seemed to mean getting stoned and looking for crocs in a turgid river. We found some very quickly and combined with the negative effects of the powerful top end marijuana, I spent a lot of time quivering in the closest to centre of the small boat that I could. The huge crocs were constantly submerging and who knows what was going on under us. The dudes seemed to think this was fun. I didn't film too much of this for fear of rocking the boat.

These prehistoric creatures are best seen in dodgy Australian romantic comedies, safely doing their evil thing on large screens. A lot of the top end is a bit like this. The beach looks lovely – but sorry there's stingers and salt water crocs everywhere. Let's go for a walk. I wouldn't do that – the wild buffalo. That water hole looks inviting – sorry, etc. etc.

But just before we leave Alice Springs, let's go to the airport. This location is a good example of the odd atmosphere around Alice. It's been the location of a surprising amount of action. Wendy Georgetti Renkes is an ex-flight attendant who used to work for Connellan Airways, that flew out of Alice in the 'seventies. Wendy's Alice Springs story was something that she told

Wendy Georgetti Renkes on left.

Wendy Georgetti Renkes: I loved the top end because they are such characters. We used to go to all these cattle stations and they were tough, tough men. I don't think I met a nasty one ever. The conditions up here are appalling. You know, the heat is stifling. And a lot of them in those days didn't have air conditioning at all. And they were running cattle. It was hot, dirty, dusty. It was a heck of a job. But they all loved it. You'd never get them out of it. And I can sort of see why. There are women up here that do do it. And there are a couple of women who actually own stations. And they are tough ladies, believe me, that hasn't changed.

me when I was working on one of the many documentaries I've made over time. It never quite made it to air but I think it's worth telling. Wendy was born in the UK, and ended up in Australia, going on to become a flight attendant for Ansett and Qantas. She loved the 'sixties 'hostie' life and talked about it with zest in a still-strong upper class English accent. She seemed out of place in the Northern Territory and often talked about it like it was the end of the earth. But with some affection. When she worked at Connellan Airways in the 'seventies, it was such a small airline that she designed her own uniform – which had to be brown to match all the dust that gets all over everything.

Connellan Airways was the sort of business where everyone knew each other and Wendy got to know the owner's son, Roger Connellan, so well that they got engaged. He was a handsome young pilot and it was a romance that could have made a good plot for a pulp fiction novel. Except for the ending.

On January 5, 1977, a disgruntled former employee of Connellan Airways stole a plane and flew it into the company's hangar at Alice Springs Airport, killing himself and four others. It was the first known case of a suicide attack by a pilot in Australia and a rare event in this country. Wendy happened to be off duty, showing some visitors around the local gap when a car pulled up and took her to the airport.

Wendy: This poor guy came over and said, 'Wendy are you alright?' And I said, Yes, but what's wrong? And he said, Roger has been killed. And that's how my life changed. I still get a bit teary. After all these years. I just stood in shock, and started to cry. And someone said, 'Get her out of here.'

next one! Oh, golly, gosh. Tim Giorgetti! God bless his heart. He killed himself. He shot himself. And though nobody knows why. Never will anyway, they were all unusual men. Most of them were very talented at what they did. But very unusual. They didn't always adhere to the pilot image which is strong and steady.

It's hard to transcribe the way that Wendy told me this story. But I've done my best. It's a cliché, but real life is stranger than fiction.

It became known in the papers as the Connellan Air Disaster and was a big news story for a while, then forgotten. After she picked herself up, Wendy continued to fly, working for Qantas on the international run. On overseas flights in those days, there was a single female hostess. They were a mix of cocktail waitress and toilet cleaner, but Wendy loved the lifestyle and the people. Especially pilots. This is where the pulp fiction plot goes really strange.

> **Wendy**: All the girls (hostesses), particularly in Ansett, were determined to marry pilots. They are relatively well paid. And when you're on the ground, you socialise with them because you're in a strange place. I always went to the pilots' quarters because I love their company and because I love to talk flying. I had a go at flying myself. And that's why I ended up with three of them. But they all had sticky ends, unfortunately. It's been very turbulent times. Roger was the first one. And after his death, I joined Qantas and met Peter Dart, an ex-air force pilot. He was a very good looking man. Unfortunately, he had a booze problem, which is a bit sad. Oh my God, I forgot the

SCANDAL RADAR

The 1970s saw a high number of hijackings – usually for political causes or ransom – and Australia was not immune from this phenomenon. In 1972, as an Ansett Australia flight was descending into Alice Springs airport, Miloslav Hrabinec entered the cockpit with a sawn-off shotgun and announced "this is a hijack". In typical Australian laconic style, the pilot said he was too busy landing the plane to talk, and told him to go and sit down. After landing in Alice Springs, Hrabinec – who had neither political or financial motives – announced he wanted to hijack the plane, transfer to another smaller plane, and then be flown to a remote location, where he would parachute out, see how long he could survive in this remote location, and then commit suicide. An unusual request. During the plane transfer, undercover police managed to shoot and wound Hrabinec, after which he ran off to a nearby ditch and fatally shot himself.

AU REVOIR AUSTRALIE

MUSIC
* *World Traveller*, OneHeadJet
* *La Javanaise*, Serge Gainsbourg
* *Islands in the Stream*, Kenny Rogers and Dolly Parton
* *Waterloo*, Abba

STAY
Sorry, but I love the airport hotel at Changi Airport. In fact the whole of Changi Airport appeals to the futuristic part of my id.

EAT
Plane food is getting better, that's about the best I can say. What happened to all that food and that whole associated industry during the recent interruptions to service?

POINTS OF INTEREST
What just happened to the world!! It's a little too interesting. Let's just block it out with some valium and a glass of average wine. Take off, sit back, feel slightly nervous, and enter the long flight zone. It's nowhere near as comforting as the car zone.

Dear fellow travellers. I am very grateful for your company – especially if you've got all the way here. It's been quite a journey. It was not what I expected when I set out from the nation's capital all those years ago. It was not so long ago I looked out the window and speculated that Australia didn't seem very different to the place I'd grown up in as a child. The cars were slightly different, there were more people of different ethnicities, but the general feel was similar. Putting this all together has made me think again. It's how life goes. Who would have thought a song like 'Islands in the Stream' by Kenny and Dolly, that I loathed when young, would turn out to be one of my favourite travelling songs?

But that is the joy of travel, the unexpected. Australia has changed, I've changed, we've all changed. Some of it for good, some of it not so good. Rob McComb from the Triffids told me that the body itself changes quite a lot over time.

Rob McComb, the Triffids: Some of your eye lenses stay the same or something like that. All the cells in your body change over pretty regularly anyway. But not the brain cells. That's right. So God, if I've still got the old brain, we're in trouble Greg!

It's been a joy talking with all the people for this book (well just about all of them). They give me hope and I hope they do the same for you. We happen to be at Alice Springs, the crossroads of Australia. We're also at an airport. Looking at screens in the departure lounge and the exotic range of things crossed out in signage I realise –

maybe the world *has* changed since we set out. You could almost say dramatically. There's been some pretty wild turbulence out there. But the roads into Alice are now all sealed. The airport tarmac here is long enough for huge jets to land. It's so tempting to get on a flight. What are we waiting for!

I think it might be the odd feeling of being on a long haul flight again, but I find myself speculating about the world below. Nations and citizens. What does it all really mean? Is Australia a thing? If you look at time lapse maps of the globe that we fly over, you can see how quickly things change. Let's not go back as far as Gondwanaland, but the more recent human past. People moving about, walking round the edges of continents, making amazing voyages across vast seas in tiny boats. Australia itself was a collection of different language, social and nation groups for a long long time. Across the water the Asian countries shift their allegiances relentlessly. We pass over the Middle East, a mind numbing history, written in the Bible, the Koran, hieroglyphs, bones. We are on our way to Europe. Why? Because due to the recent laws of the Eurovision song contest Australia is now part of Europe. Yes, just before our English masters Brexited the European Union, Australia joined the Eurovision song contest. It seems a lifetime away. The year 2015.

The odd thing is, I might just know one of the parties responsible for this geographical anomaly. You've seen Paul Clarke in an earlier chapter, posing with me in front of my brother Steve's green panel van. We've worked together on many odd projects, including the *Bottle Man* film and various documentaries of the Australian cultural entertainment variety. This man has Irish heritage. I don't want to be culturalist, but there's an attribute often bestowed on these people. It's called the gift of the gab, or blarney, or something. Anyway, you know what I'm talking about? This man has it.

I have noticed that every year, excepting those where coronavirus reeks havoc on

the globe, Paul slips off to Europe with a team from SBS, to the country that holds the Eurovision contest. That is the country that the previous year's winner resides in. To some, this may seem like an amazing lurk. But let's hear from the man himself.

Paul Clarke: My job is to take artists to Eurovision and kind of lead a team over there. You produce the staging of your act. So each Eurovision Song is bespoke, in its style. And it's got someone like me in the background saying, we need more purple lights, or we need more dancers or more nearly naked male bodies. There's at least forty-two people like me, making these calls at Eurovision. And their producers have to work with that. Because that's their version of European unity. They're bringing everybody's opinions in. I felt like I knew all about music coverage. And then I walked into this Olympic Theatre in Moscow. And they had aggregated 70 per cent of the world's LED lights in this room.

It was galactic in its scale visually. And yet, you had some of the most strange little artists and songs from Europe, coming into contact with some of the greatest technicians and the lighting products in entertainment in the world. And they're putting out one huge show, which rates more than the Superbowl. It's the biggest live music show in the world.

But how did Australia become part of this LED-filled Eurovision song contest?

Paul Clarke: I started to make friends with some of the Eurovision bosses. And it turned out that they were just like the people that I'd grown up with at the ABC in Australia. In the ABC TV Entertainment department, these kind of older camp guys, generally. Who had a career in dance shows. These really great impresarios, like Michael Shrimpton, who ran *Countdown*. People with taste and flair, and the ability to know what an audience needed. Well, it was those guys that were running the show, except they just spoke with Norwegian accents. So we became friends. They were fascinated that Australia wanted to send a commentary team, and we sent Julia Zemiro and Sam Pang. I've never seen artists respond to anybody as quick as Julia. And Sam's job was to ask stupid questions, and just pretend that he was on the way to the Brownlow medal and had taken a wrong turn somewhere. And it worked really well, it was heart versus head with the two of them. Anyway, they loved what we did. We were sort of taking the piss out of it, but enjoying it. And gradually, we just tried to extend our influence. So each year, we were trying to push it a little bit further. And then in 2015, they allowed us to actually have an artist in there.

But once Australia officially became a European song contest participant – wasn't there a reaction?

Paul Clarke: Yeah, there was a lot of that. It's a show where the publicity is driven online, and it's full of bloggers. There's a lot of fans who are just absolute trainspotters. And some of them had visceral reactions to Australia being part of it. About 20 per cent thought it was a really good thing and 80 per cent thought it was the end of the world. It took a little bit of navigation to kind of get through that. But I think the management at the time, could see the opportunity. And they could see that there was really something in this and that it didn't matter that most of the people hated it, it was going to get press.

It did turn a bit ugly when a Ukrainian draped an Australian flag flashed his arse on stage. He was almost doing a 'browneye'

– a very Australian sport in the 'seventies. He turned out to be some kind of British Nazi ranter. The SBS Australian commentator Joel Creasey was forced to use some colloquialisms. But It turned out to be one of those – any press is good press – situations in Australia's favour. J.K. Rowling even commented about it on Twitter.

J.K. Rowling@jk_rowling: Apparently the Australian commentator called @surieofficial's stage invader 'some absolute cockhead' and I don't want to hear another word about Australia being in #Eurovision ever again.

Things settled down. And as I write, Australia remains part of the Eurovision song contest. Now dear drivers – as we wing our way towards our newly annexed European home. Let's celebrate. We've come a long way. If Australia can be part of Europe, maybe anywhere can be part of anywhere? The world can live as one.

EPILOGUE

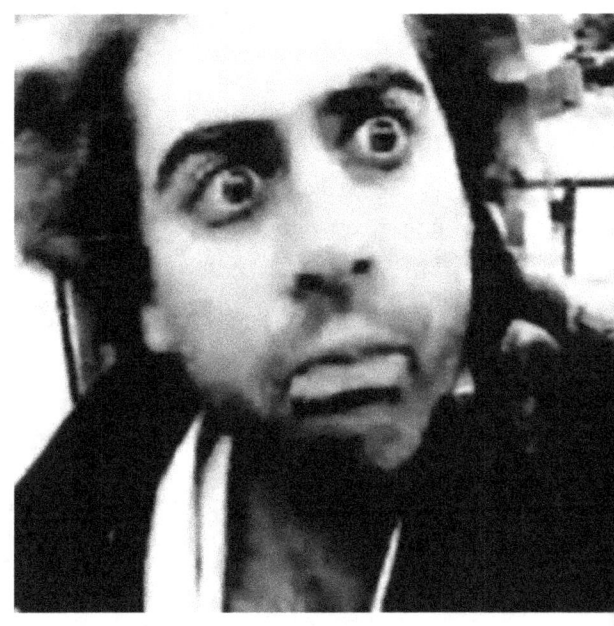

We've come to the end of our travels. Why is the following story here? If I continue to write the next book, it will all make sense. I wrote this story many years ago, it was printed on the inside cover of the Widdershins' *Ascension* (1989). This is the second part of the Bottle Man story. I am imagining that once we reach the exciting climax related here, Bottle Man might find new life, and there might even be another part. Perhaps that will set us on a new journey. Around the globe, where Australians are free to be European, make flat whites, and dispense self help. What? I don't really know how this will all work either. That's the joy of writing. Thanks for reading any of it.

THE ASCENSION OF BOTTLE MAN
by G. Appel, 1989

The day had arrived.

The day that I had feared for so long. Still, what is fear but a doorway to the unknown. I'm not sure, but the package that was forced through the slit at the top of my box, made something evil move around in my lower stomach. The colour of the envelope, the shape of the typeset, and the built in government stamp; all signalled that some thing was horribly amiss.

This was my birthday present. For this was my birthday. I was thirty-three for the record, and I knew that somehow these facts and the alignment of certain planets in my sign, were intertwined. Fate had finally become aware of my existence. I didn't like the feeling at all. Insignificance suited me,

I opened the package with trembling limbs. Nothing could have prepared me for the horror of the contents. I had thought about the possibility in the darkest recesses of my mind. I had convinced myself that I could cope. I knew that my historically long run of human vegetation might not always be fertilised. No matter how much you train for a situation, reality is a sharpened knife with an icy steel blade and a hairy brute at the end of it. I was rocked by volcanic shudders. The evil in my stomach wanted to get out. I felt the oppression of the earth's swarming masses beamed through my being. I was taken aback.

Dear Sir, (in scrawled handwriting added as an after thought — fuck-off)

It has come to our attention that you have been receiving unemployment benefits for some time now. Our records indicate 15 years continual government assistance. Firstly, may we congratulate you on achieving a regional record. Secondly, I am sure you are aware of the new policy as regards long term benefactors.

Enclosed, is a certificate of merit to honour 15 years of outstanding effort, and some material to aid you in your search for employment. The CES records indicate that you are interested in aerospace acoustics. We suggest your search should be wider, and have supplied you with 53 cards, detailing jobs in areas that we feel someone of fifteen years government support should be aiming at.

With the cards are blood sampling kits, these must be used at the time of interview by both you and your prospective employer. Three separate samples should be obtained; one to be sent to the CES, one to be sent to Social Security, and the third to be retained by yourself and produced upon demand, with a current passport and birth certificate, to our field officers.

Also contained herein: a device that looks much like a Coal-miner's helmet. Apart from making you look more presentable and emanating an aura of job experience, the "flashlight" contains a video camera that records an image visible on a screen at Social Security. This object must be worn at all times between the hours of 6am and 11pm. A current passport and birth certificate must be held in front of the "beam" on the hour. The helmet must also be worn on demand, if approached by a field officer in hours other than the above.

Card 41: Green Hills Abattoir, contact; Ron Higson. The only time an interview could be arranged was 4am, again the helmet and blood tests are imperative.

Again congratulations, your benefit has been terminated as of this date.

D. Trevicio, Acting Controller, Lewisham DSS

EPILOGUE

For a period I blacked out... When I came too, I was weak and nauseous. The room whirled around me; Cardboard, newspaper, black and white portable, half eaten Fray and Bentos, pile of leaves, glad wrap window, and the bottles. Above me, the hole in my box, the epicentre of the wheel of torment; shone the harsh rays of the outside world. I was discovered.

After the initial seven hours of uncontrollable blubbering, (I had by this stage put on the helmet and let the seeing eye rove around my abode in a shaky motion, so as D. Trevicio could get the full impact of the dreadful suffering that was wrought upon my being) I was seized by a great rage. It washed over me with a dreadful seismic force. The helmet sitting like an automated lighthouse upon my naked form, shaking as is under the impact of enormous waves. For some strange reason I felt my horn fill with angry blood and point defiantly sky-lightward. (the first for a good three years) I let the helmet slowly descend, and gaze quaking, upon the reasonably massive shaft. How could they do this to me?

Was I not trying to help these people? Was I not at the very point, where the jewel that I had been shaping and polishing all these years, was now ready for general consumption? Was I not at the apex of the mountain, after burrowing steadily upwards from the inside, while the ignorant hoards scratched and clambered and fell off on the outside. In ancient times the king

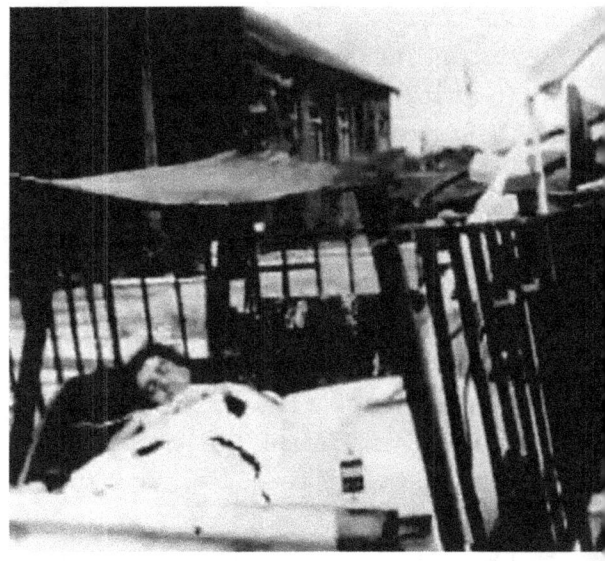

didn't receive Social Security benefits, he went out and speared you if you didn't give it to him. (or he got someone else to do it) And did the king live in a Batlow Apple container? No, he lived in a massive palace and everyone was grateful to him for accepting it. And, did he not perform the same function as myself and a lot less besides? For I am a King.

As steam blurred my vision, boiling off me, I realised that there was no way they could know the extent of their crime. Their vision was dimmed by years of ingrained minionship and narrow thoughts. The earth was already filled to bursting point with tasks that didn't need doing. Eons of repetitive motion left room only for a blind anger, directed at anyone that might not want to join in. Me, I realised my rightful place in history from an early age. (when mum took me down to the DSS and changed the lock on her door) I acknowledged that the human race had progressed, (perhaps too strong a word) and that there were many more positions available to kings than at any previous time. Do not feel guilty if you are a King, feel proud. Let the anger of the buying, selling, stamping, typing, photocopying, memo-writers be your fuel.

And at that very moment, the pride that I had kept at bay for so many years, began to swell. The temple of my soul had become tuned to my spiritual venom, causing me to vibrate wildly. I had already known that a breakthrough was imminent, that at any day my great work would reach its culmination. Today was that day.

My anger, at the overlooking of my Royalty subsided, and in its place an overwhelming feeling of zenith filled me. Love, for the people who had given me sustenance for so many years. Love, for those who had unwittingly given me the key with which to enter the door, that I had for so long been knocking upon. Love, that by my own heightened physical and spiritual nature, was at the same time sexual and psychic.

And of course, the physical aspect of love reaches its pinnacle in orgasm. My body had been a neglected vessel for so long now, that I was frightened by the feelings carousing me. I had spent so much time at the mists of my inner being that my casing was like that of an infant. (even though it looked like an apple that had remained in its box for 15 years) I was extremely sensitive. My fear was chemically changed to intense pleasure, and my spirit roamed its sanctum wildly, running from end to end grunting and spitting and slobbering. And of course, all the while the crown upon my head was copping an eyeful.

The physical aspect of orgasm is ejaculation, (or the female equivalent, and here I draw a complete blank. sad but true) The jewel contained in the crown upon my head, (by now thoroughly steamed over but regularly wiped clean by a flailing limb) was given a blast by the cream cleanser. However, when the physical is infused by the psychological, the moment is transcended. There was so much power in this one animal exodus, that the barrier between skin and thought was altered: electronically, chemically, spiritually, atomically. My self love was channelled through space and time, and became a love of everything that was not myself (a common feeling that I have in the morning, magnified a thousand-fold) I embraced all.

And now it becomes difficult to render the printed word understandable. The I becomes we. (I will still use "I" for the sake of ease, and my own acknowledgement of my own achievement; since no one else is about to do it)

I feel I am outside the box, the body, the earth, the universe. I look upon them with a new vision, that perceives the physical as only a small sector of the whole. One channel on a mighty television set. A light yellow patch on

EPILOGUE

a heavenly spectrum, that continues well past the infra-red and the ultra-violet, The box incinerates into itself. The helmet goes rocketing off into the cosmos.

My naked form is now full of many naked forms. Shapes and tones represent the myriad of personality aspects. I see my mother talking to Don Lane, commenting about the positive and negative points of his late night show. A mouth (mum) kisses a long slender penis (Don) and bites the testicles, covered by greying hair with a dramatic part to the left. Don's eyes are huge Wheels of Fortune that endlessly stop on Bankrupt, to reveal a totally bald Bert Newton. Perhaps I watched a little too much television during my years in the wilderness,

The sexual aspect of my sign has been returned to me from childhood. Indeed the sensual reality of the entire universe is revealed through my new eyes. And I'm enjoying myself immensely. A baby in a bath of warm mud.

The female half of sexuality; softness, wetness, emotion and reproduction, joins my long impotent hardness and loneliness. The sheer expanse and energy of the cosmos is within me. The two sexualities caress and repel each other. An endless cycle of power.

I am inside Julio Iglasias's well salivated form. I have his sexual knowledge. (I sing a few Latin phrases in a tremulous high pitched voice) I am Priscilla Presley, as Julio enters me with the honed caresses of a man who has made love four times a day, to thousands of different women, for forty-five years. I am Elvis, as I open one eye a knotch. Waking from a deep sleep that pulls towards the centre of the earth, and that vast quagmire of minerals and chemicals waiting to be abused. With Elvis's eyes I watch the couple writhing to a Caribbean rhythm. Waterfalls of jealousy wash over me. Julio's snakey tango is joined by a pounding back beat, to create an unpleasant cacophony not unlike dub-reggae. Then, penetrating the eternal cycle of deception and truth; violins. The cellos of acceptance, as each acknowledges the other as a part of themselves, and a part of me; the kettle drums. Perhaps I read a few too many women's magazines during my time in the darkness.

Now time and the infinite are perceived with the ease of colour and shape. I see the short history of man as a thin shaft of dark-aquamarine. The light envelops itself and explodes into stars and planets of the most incredible variety. From these physical points I can stand and look into other dimensions, and other forms of other things.(that will not permit me to put them into the English language, represented by a very narrow slit of medium-lightish olive with a four dimensional queen's head in it)

The spectrum begins to brighten and break up at one end, and darken, forming even newer hues at the other. The stars hurtle towards the centre. And I am momentarily at a loss for words...

INDEX

A
Abbott, Tony (Prime Minister) 28, 30
Adamson, Chris 54
Alberti, Susan 114
Alister, Paul 126
Alsop, Mark 2, 77
Anu, Christine 82
Appel, Anders 12–24
Appel, Greg 2, 3, 9, 18, 24, 42, 78, 92, 111, 173
Appel, Margaret, Stephen, Robert, David, Denis, Jan – Chapter 2 Canberra and more! 18–30
Appel, Zelie 2, 37, 42
Ashby, Don 58, 59, 60, 61, 63

B
Ball, Rick 145
Bardon, Geoffrey 161
Bates, Badger 146, 147
Belancic, Lou 70, 71
Belling, Faye 47
Ben (friend) 9
Bjelke-Petersen, Joh 120, 121
Blak Douglas 2, 10, 45, 90, 91, 156, 159, 161, 162
Braithwaite, Daryl 52
Brock, Peter 100
Brown, Steve 2, 58, 113, 125
Buckley, Justin 48, 49
Burley Griffin, Marion 30
Burley Griffin, Walter 30
Butler, Gavin 'Gus' 23, 24, 30, 54, 105, 108
Butler, Jane 105

C
Cassidy, Jill 138, 139
Cave, Nick 105, 106, 107, 108
Celotto, Mario 149
Chamberlain, Azaria 163
Chamberlain, Lindy 163
Charles, Barry 78
Clarke, Justine 3, 151

Clarke, Paul 2, 35, 169, 170, 171
Coates, Ivan 38, 39, 40, 135
Connellan, Roger 165
Corris, Peter 109
Cottingham, Arielle 83
Coupe, Stuart 50
Creasey, Joel 171
Crowe, Russell 114, 144, 145
Cruise, Tom 145

D
Dalton, Michael See 'Blue' (Michael Dalton)
Dart, Peter 166
Dekker, Desmond 135
d. Mather, Asma 147
Doyle, Jim 127, 128
Drew, Robert 109
Dunn, Jamie (The Nambour Song) 130

E
Erwin, Kerrie 69

F
Farnham, John 15
Fesl, Eve 126
Fran 67
Frank (cousin) 19
Fraser, Malcolm (Prime Minister) 27
Freeman, Howard 51, 52

G
Garner, Helen 109
Georgetti Renkes, Wendy 164, 165
Giorgetti, Tim 166
Green, Frances 2, 3, 13, 37, 38, 113, 159
Green, Monica 13
Grunden, John 61
Grunden, Joyceylen 61

H
Hart, Pro 146, 147
Hawke, Bob (Prime Minister) 28, 29, 31
Hawke, Hazel 29, 31
Hines, David 105, 106, 107, 108, 109
Hines, Marcia 33, 42
Hogan, Paul 29

Howard, John (Prime Minister) 31
Howard, Julie 71
Hrabinec, Miloslav 166
Huda 'the Goddess' 85
Hume and Hovell (historical) 45
Hurley, David (Governor–General) 68, 69

I
Ireland, David 108

J
John, Elton 17, 31, 120, 131
Jokovich, Eddy 2, 27, 28, 29, 109, 155, 156
Joye, Col 49

K
Kapsimallis, Dimi 71
Kelly, Paul 50
Kilbey, Steve 19, 23, 52, 53
King, Bernard 126
Kit and Les (family friends) 19
Kotchef, Ted 143
Kwai, Ajak 111, 117

L
La Rovere, Esther 148
Leyland Brothers 83

M
Marx, Jack 143, 144, 145
McAllister, Wayne 126
McCabe, Bernie 137
McCabe, Tom 35, 135, 137, 138
McComb, Rob 7, 155, 168
Meldrum, Molly 41
Menke, Brett 59
Mihelakos, Mary 155
Milat, Ivan 13
Miles, Grant 114
Milne, Bruce 155
Moffat, Allan 100
Morrison, Scott 7

N
Newton-John, Olivia 29
Nicholson, Auntie Barbara 69, 70
Norman, Greg 29
Norton, John (historical) 15

O
Ogden, John 160
O'Hagan, Jack (historical) 33, 42
O'Keefe, Johnny 49
Oliver, Jesse 83, 84
O'Neil, Stephen (Hairy) 24
Owen, Brad 34, 35, 100, 101, 102, 156

P
Pang, Sam 171
Pascoe, Bruce 59, 60
Peacock, Amanda 2, 36, 37, 41, 64, 72, 75
Pickworth, Simon 59
Plibersek, Tanya 27, 28
Podmore, Alan 47
Presley, Elvis 120, 177
Pung, Alice 2, 111, 112, 113, 115, 116, 117
Pung, Kuan 112, 116

Q
Queen Victoria 15

R
Rafalowicz, Harry 114
Rentell, Anne Louise 66, 68
Ritchie, Tim 76
Rogers (Kenny) and Parton (Dolly) 168
Rowling, J.K. 171
Rudd, Kevin 129
Rudd, Van 116

S
Sands brothers 91
Scaley (friend) 23
Schinella, Mick 148
Sello, Lancelot (friend) 38
Sewell, Hamish 129, 130
Shrimpton, Michael 170
Simpilcio 126
Stephens, Henri 68, 69, 70, 72

Stevens, Cat 7, 12
Sting 9, 20
Streep, Meryl 163
Summer, Donna 74
Swan, Wayne 129

T

Tangey, Chris 163
Taranto, Claudia 2, 71
Taylor, Neil 116, 117
Tom and Jill 75
Treagar, Richard 114
Trough Man 74, 75, 76, 77, 79
Trump, Donald 38, 157

V

Vanda (Harry) and Young (George) 42
Vergona, Lee 155
Vidgin, Jack 76

W

Walker, Clinton 40, 51, 107, 108, 109, 120, 121, 122
Wallner, Bruce 66
Walsh, David 138
Ward, Juliet 13, 20, 27, 50, 64, 142
Waye, Gordon 150
Wheelan, Justin 48
Whyte, 'Bushy' 148, 150
Wild, Sam 33, 34, 53
Wilson, Cec 62
Wilson, Naomi 59, 62
Wooley, Leigh 138
Wotherspoon, Gary 77

Y

York, Susanna 131
Young, John Paul 41, 42, 89, 90

Z

Zee Khan, Zohab 82
Zemiro, Julia 171

www.ingramcontent.com/pod-product-compliance
Lightning Source LLC
Chambersburg PA
CBHW080849020526
44118CB00037B/2320